MW00562994

PRAISE FOR *PARENTS IN RECOVERY*

"The greatest achievement of my life has been the honor and responsibility of being a sober father. Sobriety has allowed me to be fully present, accountable and vulnerable to the people that I love and treasure the most; my children, Chris Jr., Samantha and Drew. Heather and I are incredibly blessed to walk this journey together. The greatest achievement of my life has been the honor and responsibility of being a sober father. Sobriety has allowed me to be fully present, accountable, and vulnerable to the people that I love and treasure the most: my children, Chris Jr., Samantha, and Drew. Heather and I are incredibly blessed to walk this journey together. Sarah Allen Benton addresses every aspect of being a parent in recovery. Regardless of your recovery or parenting stage, she offers a 'first of its kind' navigation and motivational tool from the personal lens of clinician, educator, and parent. This is a book that you will keep and refer to again and again." **—Chris Herren, founder of Herren Project, Herren Talks, and Herren Wellness, author of *Baskteball Junkie***

"Demystifying a field shrouded in mystery and misconception, Sarah Allen Benton writes clearly about the nature of substance use disorders, the recovery process, and the blessing of going deeply. More than just a recovery book, it provides gentle guidance for parents that can benefit those in recovery . . . or not." **—Diana Clark, president of O'Connor Professional Group, author of *Addiction Recovery: A Family's Journey***

"Recovery has been the gift that has allowed me to be present in my three children's lives, but navigating parenting as a person in recovery is complex and stressful. Sarah Allen Benton's book provides a beautiful and helpful guide to this very often experienced but rarely discussed segment of parents."**—Greg Williams, filmmaker of *The Anonymous People*, *Generation Found*, and *Tipping the Pain Scale***

PARENTS IN RECOVERY

Navigating a Sober Family Lifestyle

Sarah Allen Benton

ROWMAN & LITTLEFIELD
Lanham • Boulder • New York • London

Published by Rowman & Littlefield
An imprint of The Rowman & Littlefield Publishing Group, Inc.
4501 Forbes Boulevard, Suite 200, Lanham, Maryland 20706
www.rowman.com

86-90 Paul Street, London EC2A 4NE

British Library Cataloguing in Publication Information Available

Library of Congress Cataloging-in-Publication Data

Names: Benton, Sarah Allen, author.
Title: Parents in recovery : navigating a sober family lifestyle / Sarah Allen Benton.
Description: Lanham : Rowman & Littlefield, [2024] | Includes bibliographical references and index.
Identifiers: LCCN 2024010913 (print) | LCCN 2024010914 (ebook) | ISBN 9781538181898 (cloth) | ISBN 9781538181904 (ebook)
Subjects: LCSH: Parents—Alcohol use. | Alcoholics—Family relationships. | Children of alcoholics. | Temperance.
Classification: LCC HV5132 .B468 2024 (print) | LCC HV5132 (ebook) | DDC 362.292/3—dc23/eng/20240412
LC record available at https://lccn.loc.gov/2024010913
LC ebook record available at https://lccn.loc.gov/2024010914

∞™ The paper used in this publication meets the minimum requirements of American National Standard for Information Sciences—Permanence of Paper for Printed Library Materials, ANSI/NISO Z39.48-1992.

To Josh and Eve

Contents

Introduction

PARENTING IS HARD.

Recovery is hard.

Both are impossible to prepare for before experiencing them. Many know in advance that parenting brings many challenges: sleepless nights, never-ending childcare, ongoing accountability, lack of alone time, uncertainty about parenting decisions, and the responsibility of being a role model. Many also speak fondly of the many blessings: unconditional love, the joy of watching children grow and develop, deep connection, the feeling of meaning and purpose and motivation to be a better person.

This is not a book about "how" to parent. It is also not a book about "how" to get sober. Instead, it is intended to be a guide for parents in recovery (PIRs) from substance use disorders (SUDs) that provides insight and strategies for coping with the many unique, and not so unique, challenges they may face. It is also intended to give the loved ones of PIRs an inside look at this world and explain why certain changes and behaviors are necessary for PIRs to maintain long-term recovery.

So, how many parents are in this situation?

- 46.3 million people 12 years old and older (or 16.5% of the population) met the *DSM-5* criteria for having an SUD in the past year, including 29.5 million people who were classified as having an alcohol use disorder and 24 million people who were classified as having an SUD not involving alcohol.[1]

- Only 10.8 percent of those 12 or older who needed substance use treatment actually received it.[2]
- 74.2 million parents have had an SUD[3] and 1 in 8 children 17 years old and younger live in a household with a parent who has had an SUD at some point in the past.
- One in 10 children (7.5 million) lived in households with at least one parent who had an alcohol use disorder in the past year.
- 1 in 35 children (2.1 million) lived in a household with at least one parent who had an SUD not involving alcohol.[4]

On a bright note, it is encouraging that 7 in 10 (72.2% or 20.9 million) adults who have ever had an SUD consider themselves to be in recovery.[5] Given that there are no current statistics on how many *parents* are actually in recovery, combining these statistics would indicate there are about 7 million PIRs in the United States. The number of lives that they impact is immeasurable.

While these PIRs share similarities, all have unique experiences, which may lead them to wonder if they are alone in their uncertainty. Parents recovering from an SUD are complex and dynamic individuals who bring their own nuances to the parenting process. They spend much of their early recovery focused on preventing their own relapse, learning to regulate their emotions, creating new social networks and addressing underlying mental health issues.

Many patterns and common characteristics of these parents have yet to be fully explored in the current literature. What may feel truly unparalleled and even isolating are actually shared connections. This book includes stories of PIRs, including those who:

1. Became sober before having a child(ren)
2. Became sober after having a child(ren)
3. Were initially sober when they had a child(ren) and then relapsed but became sober again
4. Had a child(ren) when they were in active addiction, became sober, and then had an additional child(ren) when sober

Parents may also suffer from other mental health and medical conditions that can complicate the process of recovery and parenting. May those parents be honored as they have demonstrated strength, overcome obstacles, and inspired those around them. These conditions do not define individuals but are essential to who they are and how they parent.

The included narratives and quotes in this book represent the real-life stories of PIRs who have fallen, battled, healed, and ultimately triumphed in their own ways. Their length of continuous sobriety ranges from two to thirty-eight years and collectively amounts to more than 400 years. A majority of these parents are involved now and/or in the past, specifically with 12-step programs, along with other supplemental self-help groups (e.g., SHE RECOVERS, Dharma Recovery, Celebrate Recovery).

Parent Recovery Wisdom is included in the latter section of each chapter and consists of suggestions from PIRs for other PIRs. These voices of men and women in recovery from alcohol use disorder and other SUDs represent various ethnicities, ages, occupations, socioeconomic backgrounds, sexual identities, gender preferences, and family system variations. They have walked this path and are willing to share their lessons with others. The suggestions offer a buffet of options for PIRs to choose which would be the best fit. The name of each parent has been changed to respect his or her privacy. Parents not in recovery were also surveyed for a point of comparison or control group. Addiction treatment professionals have provided observations and suggestions from their work with this client population.

My recovery from an alcohol use disorder and my parenting adventure have been my life's most significant peaks and valleys. I am honored to have the opportunity to write about topics for which I have personal experience and a passion. I have included my journal entries at the end of each chapter to add a personal element. May the heartfelt narratives shared in the following pages serve as a beacon lighting the way for PIRs in both the smooth and choppy waters they navigate.

1

Recovery as a Lifestyle

"Addiction is like the glass of water that you spill onto your desk; it may seem like an insignificant amount but it seeps into everything. Therefore, recovery must do the same and involves shifts in all areas of one's life."

—Jake

Recovery: What Does It Mean?

THERE IS NOT JUST ONE ANSWER but a different response for each individual with a substance use disorder (SUD). Initially, the recovery journey involves abstinence from substances, which can feel like the most daunting part. This may include a detoxification process for some and unsupervised cessation for others. Many do not realize that the most harrowing part of transitioning from "getting sober" to being "in recovery" is the large, small, and even microscopic changes that occur in every aspect of their lives.

Removing the substance does not eliminate the underlying issues and behaviors that may have led to or fueled the addiction. The longest part of the recovery process comes after an individual stops physically using a substance(s). In this period, a person is tremendously vulnerable because the feelings, situations, and pain being numbed or avoided by the substance use return with a vengeance. Some need to go to residential treatment and transitional or sober living programs, while others engage in various levels of outpatient therapy, coaching, groups, and/ or a self-help program. There is not just one path, as illustrated here:

- "I did not go to treatment but immediately joined a 12-step group and sought out a sponsor." —Cassie, age 44, sober for 15 years, mother of a nine-year-old son
- "I entered detox from heroin, crack cocaine, cannabis, alcohol, and honestly, whatever I could get my hands on. A friend of mine was in a 12-step program that he introduced me to after detox. During my early recovery, I was in outpatient therapy while actively participating in the 12-step community." —Jackie, age 38, sober for 14 years, mother of a young son and daughter
- "Residential treatment for six months, therapeutic community, then sober living, veteran treatment, a halfway house, 12-step program, relapsed, and then back to a detox program." —Matt, age 38, sober for 10 years with a young son
- "I got sober in a 12-step program and have only used this program to maintain my sobriety. I didn't go to a treatment center or program." —Nancy, age 52, sober 31 years, mother of young adult daughters
- "12-step program initially, relapse, inpatient/residential treatment for 40 days, sober living for 12 months in a small town." —Chris, age 40, sober 16 years, father of two young daughters
- "I went to multiple (residential) treatment programs and have maintained my sobriety through a 12-step program." —Maggie, age 35, sober 15 years with a newborn son
- "9 detoxes until I stayed five days, 12-step program at ages 18 and 19 after an arrest, residential treatment five times, methadone clinic, suboxone six times, and three intensive outpatient programs." —Alex, age 43, sober 12 years, with a young daughter and son

This is just a sampling of the various methods individuals initially utilized to obtain sobriety. Some were successful on their first attempt, while others needed higher levels of care, persistence, and multiple attempts. The true miracle is how they all found their initial way toward long-term recovery, have become parents, and can reflect on that process. However, getting sober was just the beginning of their recovery journey.

Addiction is a disease of "I" and can involve many self-centered behaviors. Ironically, a successful recovery plan also begins by focusing on self—but in the form of wellness and resolving interpersonal issues. Of individuals in recovery, 54 percent report using some form of assistance (any form of treatment or social support), while the rest reported recovery on their own. Of those who sought out support, 45 percent were in self-help groups (53% of these in 12-step groups and the rest in other group options), 30 percent received formal treatment (i.e., detox, residential, intensive outpatient program), 17 percent accessed recovery support services such as faith-based help and community centers, and 9 percent used medication-assisted treatment (i.e., Vivitrol® [naltrexone], Suboxone® [a combination of buprenorphine and naloxone]). Those who needed assistance in recovery had several factors in common, including having used two or three substances, using an opioid as their drug of choice, began using before the age of 15, and/or received a mental health or SUD diagnosis by a behavioral health professional.[1] The PIRs who were interviewed each used a distinctive process consisting of both differing and sometimes similar resources.

The Substance Abuse and Mental Health Services Administration (SAMHSA) defines recovery as "A process of change through which individuals improve their health and wellness, live a self-directed life, and strive to reach their full potential."[2] This definition allows a great deal of space to interpret what this may look like. As with other severe and potentially chronic health problems, a more idealistic view of full recovery from an SUD can be conceptualized as "complete and enduring cessation of all (substance)-related problems and the movement toward global health."[3] In this context, "global" refers to the larger picture of an individual's life domains.

Recovery Domains and Phases

The Recovery Coach Academy of the Connecticut Community for Addiction Recovery (CCAR) has laid out a helpful "Wellness Plan" that identifies areas of recovery wellness, including the following: connection to the recovery community, physical health, emotional health, spiritual health, living accommodations, job/education, personal daily living management, emotional/psychological wellness, intellectual wellness, occupational wellness (can include academic and financial), and social wellness.[4] These domains reflect how successful SUD recovery is integrated into *all* aspects of life.

The recovery process also includes stages that correlate with the timeline of sobriety and the work put forth toward healing. The discussion below is intended to be an overview of familiar patterns, but variation may exist.

The first stage is "*stabilization.*" It tends to occur in the initial year of early recovery. Milestones in this stage may include understanding the disease of addiction, coping with post-acute withdrawal symptoms, not using substances when faced with stressors, learning to socialize without substances, avoiding situations (places, places, and things) that may increase chances of relapse and learning to ask for support. Jackie describes how she was limited in what she was able to address during her first year, "My emotional state was so labile the first year or so of recovery that I required clinical care and medication to stabilize me . . . my mood instability was a direct consequence of my brain transitioning from a life of constant drug and alcohol use." She also describes not being able to focus on her physical health during this time "but would dabble at times with going to the gym." Molly Ashcroft, CADC, ICADC, executive director at Innovo Detox, has observed barriers for clients in early sobriety: "Barriers are typically many more than most people would imagine and include limited social supports who are sober, not knowing how to navigate social functions with other parents, limited insight into a recovery lifestyle (which is way more than 'just not drinking or using'), struggling to learn new ways to cope with stress, and learning how to be vulnerable with their support system and asking for help."

The second stage is referred to as "*deepening.*" It commonly occurs in the second year and refers to the increase in focus and understanding of the recovery process. Some of the milestones include recognizing and correcting behaviors that no longer feel appropriate, focusing on emotional sobriety, increasing the quality of physical health, increasing the ability to tolerate distress, learning to identify feeling states, increasing commitment to recovery, and increasing the ability to address underlying mental health and medical issues. This can also be a difficult time because the novelty of the first year has worn off. "Everyone is a good sprinter. The marathon of recovery is much harder. The first few years are so hijacked by the brain that it is difficult to make the right choices," says Cody Gardner, an addiction treatment consultant.

The third stage is "*connectedness.*" It may occur in the third and fourth years of recovery. Milestones may include feeling a greater level of both joy and pain, appreciating the need to revisit earlier recovery work, establishing clear boundaries, avoiding emotional entanglements, developing consistency between inner and outer life, being open to a broader circle of friends in and out of recovery, and addressing deeper layers of relationship or mental health issues. Victoria LaMadeleine, CPC, IAPRC a certified professional coach, recommends that her clients "Take a deep look at all areas of life to determine where there needs to be more attention in recovery. I utilize a wheel of life in my sessions with clients. That will lead to pinpointing areas that they are lacking effort or overwhelmed."

The fourth stage is "*integration.*" It typically occurs in years six through ten of recovery. Milestones in this stage include having relationships based on love versus need, using recovery tools automatically, having the ability to act on self-knowledge and insight, practicing self-forgiveness, and enjoying life and finding peace. This stage is one of maintenance and flow for many. "The longer I have stayed sober, the more emotional sobriety becomes a focus. To me, emotional sobriety means being able to notice what I am feeling and reacting appropriately to those emotions," Jackie explains.

The fifth and final stage, "*fulfillment,*" refers to the characteristics of those who have been in recovery for ten years or longer. This stage is characterized by discovering and following through on life purpose, living with and knowing how to return to a sense of peace/serenity, aligning morals and actions, developing confidence in recovery rhythm, and having gratitude and pride in recovery.[5] Nancy noted, "My spiritual life has evolved over time and tremendously while my kids grew. I felt like each growing stage required me to do a different kind of spiritual work to keep me sane. The more work I did, the better I felt as a person. This is still true today."

So, what does this mean for PIRs? It indicates that on top of the many layers of responsibilities and time built into being a parent, PIRs also need to focus on maintaining balance in many other domains. Being in recovery is not just a "phase" or a limited period of time. It is how PIRs live and relate to those around them. The substance use of PIRs deeply impacted themselves and their loved ones, as it does their recovery.

Recovery Lifestyle

According to the Merriam-Webster dictionary, lifestyle is defined as "the typical way of life of an individual, group, or culture."[6] A common misunderstanding about those in recovery from an SUD is that they can exist in the world the same way they did before getting sober. Although being "abstinent" from substances without addressing other necessary components of recovery is an option, it does not result in the best outcomes for long-term recovery. Instead, "full recovery" is comparable to being part of a culture. This commonality requires a pattern of behaviors and belief systems that allow for ongoing growth and a reduced potential for relapse.

PIRs who have maintained long-term sobriety express the need to find balance in the various wellness domains, including making necessary social changes, addressing underlying mental health issues, shifting environmental factors, having a clear recovery plan, and embarking on spiritual pursuits. These efforts are baked into their lives and filter through to their family system. In other words, it is how they live. As suggested by the recovery stages, many years may be needed to attain this level of integration, but it is the ultimate goal. The process is nonlinear and involves experimentation. Many PIRs report that they have explored different behavioral schedules, spiritual practices, recovery resources, self-help meetings, sober supports, vocational/academic pursuits, and clinical services. The common theme among PIRs with long-term sobriety is an openness to ongoing growth. "We are either evolving or stagnant," affirms Violet, age 38, sober for 18 years with three children. When PIRs stumble, they are also willing to recommit to whatever area needs more attention. The benefits of the recovery lifestyle exceed simply staying sober; it can lead PIRs to excel. "The consistency in long-term recovery can often lead us to do high-level things in our lives," asserts Douglas, age 42, sober 14 years with a young son.

Sharon, age 55, who has been sober for 24 years and has a grown daughter and son, thoroughly describes her recovery lifestyle:

> *Physical:* I have adopted and grown to love a life of fitness. Setting personal goals—and surpassing them—is the best feeling in the world. I often say I wish I had known about the power of endorphins and team spirit as a teen. I may not have felt the need to pick up substances.
>
> *Psychological/emotional:* I finally got a therapist after 20+ years of recovery. I learned that the rooms and the steps are just the beginning. I needed therapy to dismantle the narrative and associated trauma of my childhood and early adult life.
>
> *Social:* A 12-step program was my place for social connection. My world has expanded because of sobriety, and I have "circles" of friends both in and outside the rooms.
>
> *Environmental:* My space reflects the care and compassion that I have for myself, and my fur babies bring me immense joy. Fortunately, my work environment has been fulfilling and supportive.
>
> *Spiritual:* I practice meditation as often as possible. When I forget to meditate, I remember to be mindful of internal and external cues. Sometimes it's as simple as just pausing to look around, take a breath, and connect with my higher power.

Fully embracing recovery as a lifestyle can also be challenging. Sheila Coleman, DSW, LMSW highlights, "To suggest to someone that they may have to change literally everything is not accepted these days. The option to substitute has become second nature rather than leaning into the discomfort of being in their own skin and working through underlying causes for substance use." However, it is important that this resistance be met with an equally convincing reflection of how important change and tolerance to distress are in this process. Sheila emphasizes that "We meet clients where they are at, but the sweet spot is knowing when to apply gentle pressure once a therapeutic rapport is established. Challenging the cognitive distortions about substance use will at least highlight the dissonance." Cody notes that just the time needed to devote to early sobriety can be a deterrent for some individuals. Vanessa Stanley, admissions counselor for Lionrock Recovery, finds that clients have difficulty finding time to engage in a recovery lifestyle when "they just want to do treatment and not change everything." Greg Williams, director of the documentary film *The Anonymous People*, describes recovery as "a process. It's not an overnight journey of awakening. In early recovery, when I was close to that chemical use, it was much more challenging. But, over time, I was able to build a new lifestyle. The power of collective good is the antidote."[7] The key is that recovery is not just about getting sober or engaging in treatment; it is about restructuring how individuals construct their lives.

Greg Williams describes several styles of connecting with the recovery culture. He describes the "acultural" style, in which individuals initiate and sustain sobriety without relationships with other individuals in recovery and do not relate to the *culture* of recovery. Others demonstrate a "bicultural" style in that they can operate within several communities of recovery, master the language and the nuances of those fellowships and also associate with "normies" or individuals not in recovery. The "culturally enmeshed" style is most common in early sobriety and involves creating a safety net or sanctuary with almost no contact with individuals not in recovery. These styles can change over time, but it is important to note that there is not necessarily one way in which to exist.[8]

Because there is not just one "treatment" for SUDs, there is room for interpretation, which is confusing for individuals or creates excuses not to engage fully. Clear treatment plans for other medical and mental health conditions have been established, leading to more consistent adherence and prognosis. In addition, minimizing and/or not believing there is an actual substance use problem is a hallmark symptom of SUDs. Cody asserts, "Addiction is a diagnosable and treatable condition. We must find the right medicine, the right dose and then take the medicine until symptoms improve." This "medicine" needs to be taken indefinitely, and it involves many wellness and lifestyle changes that will vary for each individual.

The Parenting Paradox and Imposter Syndrome

The construct of a "parent" often conjures up an image of a responsible, reliable, nurturing, and mature mother or father. The view of an individual with an SUD may be the opposite: irresponsible, unreliable, immature, and selfish. This paradox can be hard to reconcile for some PIRs, while others can better integrate aspects of themselves.

Maggie discloses,

> I honestly feel like this can be a daily struggle, a weekly struggle, or a monthly struggle depending on what I am going through. I would say it mostly works in my favor that if I am feeling overwhelmed with my daily responsibilities as a parent, I am able to remind myself that this life is something I "get" to do. At one point when I was active in my addiction, I had no hope of ever being able to be a mom or someone who a child could look up to.

Matt adds that he can get flooded with emotions thinking about how different his parenting life is from his past, mainly when he is with his friends from his youth. He explains that they sometimes "pinch themselves" reflecting on how much their lives have changed since their more irresponsible days of using. Jackie finds, "I'm incredibly perplexed at my life today when I travel with my family. Every time we're in a new state or country, enjoying each other's company and the experience of being in a new place, I am in awe that this is my life now. I don't ever feel stuck in the paradox, but I do feel a deep sense of gratitude that I was able to access recovery when I did."

In contrast, some PIRs who got sober after having children struggle with the parenting paradox in a different way. Substance use was the numbing agent they used to cope with parenting stressors. But now that that is no longer an option, some PIRs find they lack the life skills to parent effectively. Evelyn, age 53 who has been sober for 10 years and has a teenage son and daughter, reveals,

> Especially when my kids were younger, and I was in my first few years of recovery, I realized that I'm much more anxious, impatient, and short-tempered than I thought I was. Every time I felt those feelings before getting sober—and boredom was a big one too—I would numb them with alcohol. In early recovery (like the first three years), those feelings were really pointy and scary—I didn't know how to parent when annoyed, bored, upset, or overwhelmed. The paradox of feeling like a "worse" parent sober than drunk took a lot of work.

The perception that she was better able to handle parenting when using substances may have been true until she learned the necessary coping, self-care, and relapse-prevention skills while not using substances as a shortcut.

"You stop maturing at the age that you started using substances" is a common saying in the recovery community. This delay in emotional development can also influence the level of readiness and conflicting feelings PIRs may encounter when in the parenting role. It can also exacerbate the "imposter syndrome" belief system: "a psychological condition that is characterized by persistent doubt concerning one's abilities or accomplishments accompanied by the fear of being exposed as a fraud despite evidence of one's ongoing success."[9] Many PIRs were living before or after having children in reckless, dangerous, and irresponsible ways and have wrestled with viewing themselves in a positive light, regardless of being high- or low-functioning. Therefore, becoming a parent does not immediately erase past self-image because it can be deeply engrained from shame, trauma, and others' opinions.

"I remember looking at my wife and thinking 'we're just a couple of immature kids who never grew up trying to do something very adult,'" Nancy recalls. Jackie illustrates that she felt like an imposter when she would "handle the day-to-day tasks of being an adult, like paying bills, making appointments, cleaning the house, and showing up for family and friends. My ability to do the responsible, right thing was so altered when I was using that, in some ways, I just thought that was who I was. The recovery process for me was learning how to live life again because, during my active addiction, I was unable to manage life." She also volunteered as a chaperone at her daughter's field trip. She explained that she wanted to be there because her daughter had asked her and because she recalled her parents working and being unable to chaperone when she was younger. She noted that she felt different than the other "typical" volunteer parents and wondered what they would think if they knew about her past. She reflected that other parents would never look at her and think that she had been a crack cocaine user who had spent six months in jail and done unthinkable things to obtain drugs. She stuffed those memories down and jokingly stated, "Okay, let's focus on the important things to survive this field trip. Where are my nicotine pouches?" Maggie, a new mother, admits, "I struggle to think I am equipped to be a parent at times given people in my family system still bring my thoughts back to a time when I was in the height of my addiction. At times, I even second-guess myself, and imposter syndrome can creep into my psyche. I question if I am equipped to be a mother and if I have what it takes to be the best mom I can be."

This sense of imposter syndrome and guilt can impact parenting style. This seems more prevalent with parents who became sober after they had their child(ren). Evelyn initially got sober when her children were three and five and reported feeling these emotions strongly during the first six years of sobriety. "I struggled with so much shame and became a too-lenient parent as a result. I struggled with boundaries with my kids as well." Evelyn's story suggests that not working through feelings of inadequacy or setting limits can impact a parent's recovery and is crucial to address with outside support. David, age 47, has been sober for 19 years. He had two daughters from a previous marriage when he was in active addiction and has since remarried and has two younger boys who have only known him in recovery. His PIR experience is unique and affords him insight into two completely different parenting scenarios. He expresses that he feels imposter syndrome with his older daughters: "All the time, I feel like because of past behaviors and choices, and the way that time in my life is received/portrayed, I have lost credibility as a parent." However, he has a chance with his younger boys to have a new parenting journey with more confidence and belief in himself.

Many first-time parents in and out of recovery may not feel prepared initially and have an expected sense of imposter syndrome. In contrast, some PIRs feel increased trust in themselves and a fierce sense of protection for their child, which trumps their inexperience and pasts. "I know I live a completely different life. But since becoming a parent, everything is based on considering my son," Matt reflects confidently. His recovery has been strengthened since becoming a father and having someone fully dependent on him. Laura, age 64, sober 38 years and with two adult sons, reported feeling immense gratitude for her recovery as a parent and expressed that "My children knew boundaries and love. . . . As a sober parent, I was able to share some of the things I did right and some I did wrong."

Parent Recovery Wisdom

The following strategies for PIRs from both PIRs and addiction treatment professionals highlight ways to create a recovery lifestyle in various domains. Lifestyle strategies can involve deeper integration than self-care strategies. Some are listed exactly as the PIRs stated to capture the precise tone and message they wanted to communicate. The following suggestions are meant to provide options and are not intended to be used in their entirety.

Recovery Program

"Recovery is a verb."

—Recovery expression

- Find a self-help program that "moves" you.
- Learn to navigate a world that caters to those who drink and use substances.
- Prioritize your recovery first, and the rest will fall into place.
- Learn and take the time to implement the suggestions of the self-help program that you have chosen to commit to. That is the roadmap for recovery.
- Create a solid sobriety foundation; then taking on other responsibilities becomes achievable.
- Make a shift in one life domain, feel the impact and allow that momentum to carry over to others.
- Remain open to the idea that recovery penetrates every domain of your life and that the transformations occur over time.

Physical and Psychological

"Getting into a routine of moving your body, walking, stretching, exercise of any kind will help your mood, your cravings, and your overall outlook."

—Jill Griffin, LCSW, LADC

- Create a consistent behavioral daily and weekly schedule.
- Treat your mind and body with respect.
- Learn to communicate with healthcare providers about your SUD and mental health history.
- Find healthy and safe ways to take medications as prescribed.
- Prioritize physical and mental health as part of recovery.
- Engage in some form of personal growth that honors you.

- Allow psychological wellness to become deeply connected to your recovery.
- Change the old routines and patterns that precipitated the urge to use your substance of choice.
- Integrate recovery activities into your calendar and schedule.
- Commit to a recovery routine that may have some variation but is consistent.
- Strive for balance.

Environmental

"My home is my safe haven; this is not negotiable."

—Sharon

- Create a home environment that outwardly represents your recovery and wellness goals.
- Eliminate or minimize having any alcohol or substances in your home.
- Establish a sense of organization.
- Make changes in your home to accommodate recovery.
- Create a home that feels comforting and secure.

Social

"It's important to have a tribe in recovery, especially in the beginning. I wouldn't be where I am today without all the fellowship and support I received from individuals who entered their recovery journey before me. It's been one of the greatest gifts I've received in recovery, connecting with individuals, and allowing them to truly see me—the good, the bad, and the ugly. As my recovery journey has evolved, I make an effort to have face-to-face time with my closest friends and keep in contact with them regularly."

—Violet

- Surround yourself with others who have the type of recovery that you admire.
- Be of service in the community but also in your family system.
- Allow others into your recovery process.

- Spend time with other parents who are living a recovery lifestyle or who respect yours.
- Do your best to have your family and friends understand the importance of your recovery and self-help meetings (if they do not, then still press on).
- Make changes based on your recovery needs and not on others' opinions.

Spiritual

> *"To me, my spiritual condition is the single most important aspect of maintaining a program of recovery. I have always had a belief in God, even when I was in active addiction. I have found that my relationship with God and the universe has changed over the years. My rituals and routines around prayer and meditation have definitely been affected by parenthood as my time is no longer my own, especially when my children were younger. I have learned to be flexible and continue seeking a spiritual connection no matter what my life circumstances are at the time."*
>
> —Jackie

- Find some form of spirituality or connection with the universe that can be integrated into everyday life.
- Find out what allows you to be in tune with yourself because "everywhere you go, there you are."
- Create time or moments in your day to connect with your spiritual source.
- Never stop growing. Ever.

Personal Journal Entries

I had seven years of recovery before I became a mother, and I am grateful to have had that time to become grounded in the lifestyle. I gradually figured out this way of life over time and through my own trials and errors. These gratitude journal entries demonstrate how recovery wellness was woven into my existence.

June 30, 2013—Eve, six months old

Gratitude: Amends process, peace in my heart versus resentment, friends, sobriety

July 1, 2013

Gratitude: Opportunity for amends, practice needing to restrict reactions with Eve [my daughter], grateful to learn new ways to parent, stability and ability to grow

July 3, 2013

Gratitude: Balanced schedule, opportunities to help others, friendships, forgiveness, love, Eve's happiness

July 4, 2013

Gratitude: Sober friends, meetings, support system, accumulated knowledge of sobriety

December 25, 2013

Gratitude: Family, home, emotions passing

December 28, 2014—Eve, 1 year and 11 months old

Gratitude: Eve's intuitiveness, Josh's [my husband] patience, my home, hope, self-help meetings

December 28, 2014

Gratitude: Peace, respite from pain, mindfulness, understanding, compassion

December 31, 2014

Gratitude: Sobriety, emotional security, unconditional love

January 6, 2015—Eve, three years old

Gratitude: Running, God, ability to change, starting over

January 23, 2015

Gratitude: Sober escapes, movies, parental "breaks"

2

The Intrinsic and Extrinsic Parenting Continuum

> *"Parenting has come so naturally, I just feel like I was born to do this."*
> *"Why do other parents make this look so easy, while I am struggling so much?"*
> *"I am uncomfortable when people tell me to 'enjoy every moment, it goes by so quickly' because I struggle to do that."*
> *"I have never felt a greater sense of purpose than being a parent."*
>
> —PIRs

These comments show the extraordinary disparity in parenting experiences. Some parents feel a sense of pride that they are floating through the process, while others feel embarrassed to admit that they are drowning. Parents also vary in their level of expressiveness about the positive and negative aspects of parenting—but the silence around this topic can be deafening.

Today's parents are flooded with information from social media, books, magazines, blogs, and podcasts, making it impossible to know where to turn for the most trusted information. Parenting trends ebb and flow over time and are hard to keep up with or to relate to—attachment parenting, conscious parenting, positive parenting, free-range parenting, tiger parenting, and more. Author and journalist Jennifer Senior recognized this missing piece of academia when she took on the massive project of consolidating existing parenting studies and integrating them with interviews. In her book, *All Joy and No Fun*, she observes, "But the truth is, there's little even the most organized people can do to prepare themselves for having children. They can buy all the books, observe friends and relations, review their own memories of childhood. But the distance between those proxy experiences and the real thing, ultimately, can be measured in light-years."[1]

Past and present research in the field of developmental psychology also impacts parenting trends and culture. Dr. Diane Baumrind is considered a pioneer in the study of parenting styles. She published research in the 1970s[2] and early 1990s[3] about the impact of four parenting styles: authoritarian, authoritative, permissive, and neglectful. Additionally, psychological theories abound regarding family systems and the influence that family members have on one another.[4] While landmark research and parenting books can be informative, they have been followed by new research about even more effective parenting.

A large portion of parenting research, books, and articles focus on how parents impact their children. Jessica Grose, author of *Screaming on the Inside: The Unsustainability of American Motherhood*, explains, "There is just such an avalanche of information about every parenting topic, even the most educated, informed parents struggle to sift through the data. Though, in many ways, modern American parenting is easier than it used to be (we have antibiotics, motor vehicles, and indoor plumbing), it is uniquely difficult in the amount of information we get about what we're supposed to be doing and how high the stakes are made to seem about every minor decision."[5]

In contrast, much of the real-time dialogue between parents in and out of recovery is on how to fulfill the needs of their child(ren) along with their own needs. Given that parenthood is one of the most dramatic shifts in adult life, it is surprising that there are still gaps in applicable, relatable, and relevant information. Senior asserts, "Thousands of books have examined the effects of parents on their children. But almost none have thought to ask: What are the effects of children on their parents."[6] Additionally, what is the specific impact of PIRs on their children? Or the impact of children on PIRs? The only research available is on the effects of parental substance use on their child(ren). Yet there is so much to be studied and learned from these family dynamics. This information could inspire parents with SUDs to get help and encourage PIRs for the positive impacts of their lifestyle choices and changes. Simply put, the parenting experience has been rarely studied and is seemingly nonexistent regarding that of PIRs.

While research and publications are lacking, the patterns are evident. Parents fall into one of three categories of parenting experience: intrinsic, extrinsic, or hybrid. An intrinsic parent can be defined as a mother or father who adapts more easily to the parental role, demands, and identity of a parent. An extrinsic parent can be described as a mother or father who finds the transition to parenting not intuitive and has more difficulty adapting to various demands of the parenting role. A hybrid parenting experience is described as a parent who falls into each category during distinct periods or phases.

This categorization of the parenting experience creates a framework for examining influences on role integration of parents. While this relates to parents in and out of recovery, PIRs often lack clarity about the effects of their SUD and recovery. There can be a sense of healing when PIRs realize that they are not alone, that their substance use was just one of many factors impacting their parenting experience and that their recovery has benefited their family system.

Biological Clocks

> *"I have had enough therapy to understand the role that my childhood played in my addiction and all my life. I never wanted kids, not wanting to even think about my own childhood. And then as I approached my later 30s, I suddenly had this thought that I could give someone the childhood I should have had."*
>
> —Cathy, age 55 and sober 8 years before having her son

How does having a history of an SUD and being in recovery impact PIRs' maternal and paternal drives? Societal expectations surround if and when individuals "should" want to have children. But the drive to become a parent is not always innate.[7] For those with more subtle or nonexistent biological clocks, this timeline adds pressure to individuals who are single or in a partnership. People are bombarded with the statistics surrounding the increased risks of waiting to have children, such as learning that women older than age 30 have a 20 percent chance of getting pregnant, with a significant decline to only a 5 percent chance at age 40. After age 35, pregnancies are considered "high-risk," which can increase the chances of complications, developmental disabilities, and birth defects, as well as anxiety around the entire process. Meanwhile, men have decreased fertility in their late 30s and a higher risk of having a child with developmental disabilities if over age 40.[8]

Many PIRs expressed that they had always wanted to have children but that the challenges surrounding their SUD delayed the process or their ability to maintain a mature romantic relationship. Maggie, age 35 who had her son when she was 14 years sober, explains that "I just didn't have the desire. My life was filled with chaos and uncertainty, and I was barely able to care for myself. To be a parent in my eyes meant to be selfless, and I was the opposite of that in my addiction." Steve, age 39, who had his first child when he was 15 years sober, believes his desire and process were delayed because of relationship issues, fear surrounding the sacrifices necessary to have a child and the question, "What if I return to being selfish?" Nancy, despite getting sober when she was 21 years old, felt that she was "years behind most of my friends" because of the time she believed alcohol had stolen from her. "I didn't think I was mature or selfless enough to have children." Tracie, age 46, whose children were 11 and 13 when she became sober, added that she always dreamed of becoming a parent and adjusted well to the process. She now "loves sober parenting" and being in the moment with her teenagers.

Some PIRs became sober at a young age, which may have sped up their readiness for becoming a parent. Violet, age 38, got sober when she was 19 years old and always wanted to have children. "I guess because that's considered the American dream, and the thought of creating a human is magical to me." Jackie, age 38, reports that she had always wanted to have children and felt ready to take on more mature life responsibilities. She explains that getting sober in her early 20s gave her time to plan out her family. Valerie, age 42, has been sober since she was 18 and has always felt more comfortable with children than adults because "they love cleaner." She felt prepared to parent from a younger age, but "Because I got sober so young, I had goals I wanted to achieve that made it harder to meet people who were 'as together' as I was."

Other PIRs never wanted to have children, but then something shifted, and they changed their minds. Cassie, age 44 and 6 years sober when her son was born, admits that she did not want to have children mainly because she did not think she would be "good at it." However, meeting her husband in recovery and seeing how much he loved children led her to want to have a child with him. David, age 47, was in active addiction when his two daughters were born and then ten years sober when his son was born, discovered that "after years in sobriety, I wanted a second chance to be a better, more present father." Cathy adds that while she had never wanted children due to her traumatic childhood and SUD, "I'm so grateful I didn't miss motherhood though, because it's the best thing that ever happened to me."

The Intrinsic Parenting Experience

> *"I would describe myself as intrinsic, and the only way I can accurately describe it is that when my son was born, I had an instinct that knew exactly what he needed and how to do it."*
>
> —Maggie

Maternal and paternal instincts are often viewed as inherent traits—inborn and natural responses of a parent to their child. Dr. Catherine Moss, psychologist and professor of medical psychology at Columbia University Medical Center, has found several other variables that influence what may appear to be pure instinct, including "learning on the job through instruction, good role models, and observing what works and doesn't with each child."[9] She has found that parental instinct can be learned over time. Dr. Dana Dorfman, a child and adolescent psychologist, lists a confluence of factors that impact intrinsic parents' ease with their role, including past experiences, temperament, and attachment styles.

A mother's brain chemistry and hormones change during pregnancy with shifts in estrogen and oxytocin—the bonding hormone. Research indicates this is also true for fathers and adoptive parents after birth. They experience heightened levels of oxytocin, serotonin, and dopamine during the transition to parenthood, which increases from engaging in bonding activities.[10] This can help explain why biological mothers, fathers, and adoptive parents may have similar instant connections with their children.

In an Australian study, mothers and fathers were asked if the skills needed to be a good parent come naturally to most people: 58 percent of mothers younger than age 25 endorsed this statement, while three-quarters of mothers aged 45–54 rejected it. Fathers younger than age

25 were evenly divided on the issue, while 58 percent of those 55 and older disagreed. The researchers concluded that people would likely alter their views of natural parenting skills as they grow older and gain experience. Maybe the saying "ignorance is bliss" applies to parenting![11]

SUDs add a confounding variable to the parenting landscape. Some of the PIRs interviewed became sober before becoming parents, others embraced sobriety after becoming a parent and several had a relapse as a parent. These factors play a part in PIRs' self-image as parents and also in their instincts and drives. Some intrinsic PIRs credit their recovery for preparing them for parenting. Jackie expressed, "I think the work I did in my recovery program helped me get to a healthy place to be able to stay present as a new parent and to not rely on my own expectations. My ability to remain flexible is more related to my recovery program. I always reflect back to my active addiction and know that I would have absolutely put my addiction ahead of anyone, including my children. It makes me so grateful that I entered parenthood as a sober woman." Maggie affirms, "My recovery has more to do with it than my active addiction. My recovery has been filled with caring for others and for myself in ways that I was incapable of even being aware of when I was drinking and using. I have had the ability to learn both my needs and the needs of others through my recovery program."

A recovery lifestyle and a healthy social circle can also be positive influences. Steve relates, "I have a lot of friends in recovery and was around them and their children. I picked up some of the things they were doing and even had a role with their children." In some cases, PIRs can hyperfocus on their child's needs. Valerie explains that she struggles to make time for herself because of her extreme focus on caring for her children, which is problematic for her as a PIR—when it is imperative to "put your oxygen mask on before putting it on your children."

PIRs who became sober after becoming parents or relapsed as parents have a unique perspective on their experiences. SUDs can hijack the brains of even the most devoted parents, blocking them from being able to attune to their instincts. Molly Ashcroft, CACD, ICADC, has observed that some intrinsic parents "are living with a different kind of shame, which includes the idea of failing as a parent because they can handle most areas of parenting and yet still find a 'reason to drink and use drugs.' Parents in that space feel very much like a 'failure' and that their children will lose respect, love, and compassion for them."

Marilyn, age 63, who became sober when her children were teenagers, identifies herself as an intrinsic parent before increasing her alcohol usage and then again after becoming sober. "For me, alcoholism got in the way of my parenting, as opposed to my parenting feeding the alcohol use." Tracie expresses that she has had increased confidence around her parenting since getting sober and that "Without the shame and guilt of hangovers and physical sickness, I am able to be present and connect with my girls. I'm happy, relaxed, confident, and emotionally available as a sober mother." Sharon, age 55, who embraced sobriety when her children were 11 and 16, notes, "I never lost sight of my innate ability to nurture my children. It was during the active addiction that actual parenting became unsustainable." Joan, age 43, became sober when her first daughter was 15 months old. She believes the timing of her recovery has made her more aware and able to listen to her children's needs before reacting.

Some PIRs had traumatic upbringings with a parent(s) who had an SUD and other issues. As a result, these PIRs are hyperaware of their children's needs and are fiercely protective of them. Laura, age 64, was sober before having her children. At a young age, she had to take on the role of primary caregiver in parenting her younger siblings. She attributes her intrinsic parenting experience to this and "wanting better for my children." Cathy felt "committed to raising my son without the emotional abuse from my own childhood. Parenting *right* from day one became this kind of healing exercise because I was giving him what I wish I'd had. It was a kind of do-over that had a fringe benefit of making me feel good about myself and the job I was doing."

Extrinsic Parenting Experience

> *"As much as I love my child and do my best to fulfill my role as his mother, it does take extra effort to do the things associated with parenting."*
>
> —Natasha, age 36, sober before having her son

While extrinsic parents may not feel the same level of intuition around parenting, they may be operating from a different biological incentive than previously believed. An instinct is an innate or unlearned response to a signal, while human drives are behavioral motivations. People do not have the same rigid instincts as animals; how they satisfy their basic needs is much more variable. For example, we have various means by which we satisfy our biological need for food such as hunting, gardening, cooking, grocery shopping, or going out to a restaurant. While the extrinsic parenting instinct can be stronger for some and weaker for others, parents can harness and redirect their drive or behaviors. Therefore, parenting can be counterintuitive and require more effort for extrinsic versus intrinsic parents, who have more alignment between their instinct and drive.

Research on new mothers found that feelings of affection for a baby may not develop until days or months after birth, leading that mother to feel a sense of shame or failure. However, their *drive* to develop those feelings was there despite the natural instinct being slower to catch up.[12] The sense of overwhelm and lack of skills is not unique to extrinsic PIRs. A study in the *Journal of the American Medical Association* found a five-year trend from 2016 to 2020, with 67.2 percent to 59.9 percent of parents not being able to cope with parenting demands for their children up to age 17.[13]

Extrinsic parents also report feeling shame that they have a healthy child(ren) and disillusionment with the parenting role, knowing others struggle with infertility. Other sources of shame include admiring parents who appear more naturally adapted and wondering what is "wrong" with themselves as extrinsic parents, feeling guilt around how hard parenting can be, resenting their child(ren), and sensing that some instinctual part of them is broken. Molly Ashcroft has found it can be effective to support PIRs with these challenges by "helping them lean into the challenge of having children and of being a parent and embracing that their experience may be different from that of others around them."

While some PIRs revealed their traumatic childhoods, others did not have the same history. Having a loving home and upbringing can be even more confusing for extrinsic parents because they witnessed their parent(s) engaging in the process with ease. PIRs who had a "super mom" or "super dad" find it all too easy to perceive they fall short in comparison. There is no perfect formula, and each parent has a unique way of doing the job. Children pick up on truth and honesty, and it can be beneficial for them to see parents face adversity, embrace it, and find ways to grow.

Jill Griffin, LADC, LCSW, offers a valuable perspective on the underpinnings of intrinsic and extrinsic parenting experiences. In her private practice, she found that "Extrinsic parent types who have more difficulty had an idea of what parenting would 'look like' and when their children do not fit that image, the parents become dysregulated. I often find that parents in recovery, especially early recovery, get knocked out of their routine easily at the competing demands of a child and find themselves outside their window of tolerance." She has also observed the signs of dysregulation that may include "disconnecting from the present, scrolling phones, or 'checking out' from the family system. In contrast, this can also include a state of hyperarousal in which parents are highly reactive, yelling at children for crying or having big emotions, or having increased anxiety themselves during difficult parenting moments." Beyond instinct, human nervous systems can also play an essential role in how PIRs manage parenting demands.

SUD-related issues can contribute to some parents identifying with the extrinsic parenting type. For some PIRs, the actual SUD interferes with parenting, while for other PIRs the issue can be a residual preoccupation with self. Stacie, age 35, became sober when her son was four and went on to have two children after she was five years sober. She points out, "I feel this way with my oldest child, whom I had when I was in active addiction and lost custody for a few years because of my addiction. My younger two I had when I was in recovery, and I had an easier time adapting. Throughout recovery, I've slowly matured and have become more confident in myself as I work on self-love and self-acceptance." She realized that at times she had been comparing herself to friends who did not have children, which made her feel "less functional." Natasha believes that having an SUD stalled her emotional development and contributed to dissonance with parenting. She explains, "I do find that the self-centered nature of my disease is something that I battle with on a daily basis." She adds that she had been in active addiction for 16 years and has now been sober for six years, which leads to an unnatural feeling in every part of her life today. Jake, age 40, who became sober before having his four children, found that he had used substances to self-medicate mood symptoms and stress. He still finds himself "consumed" in his own mind and struggling to get into the moment with his children.

Childhood trauma and a history of mental health issues can impact PIRs differently. Several intrinsic parents found that these previous experiences were a driving force toward nurturing and protecting their child(ren). Some extrinsic parents who had similar previous experiences found that they lacked a proper skill set for parenting because they did not have a healthy example. Chase, age 49, who had three daughters before getting sober and one while in recovery, relates that parenting did not come naturally to him because he did not have a role model for what "good parenting" would look like. Natasha revealed that her traumatic upbringing did not provide her with healthy influences, leading to a fear of projecting that onto her son. Jill Griffin put these responses into context, explaining that

> Oftentimes, people in recovery have trauma or emotional pain that they need to address. When a person becomes a parent, their own childhood comes into sharper focus and can reactivate childhood trauma, neglect, or chaos that they didn't recognize until they became a parent themselves. These realizations sometimes highlight relational trauma or confusion about how they were raised. It can be very difficult to hold space for a child and remain present as a parent when you are grappling with your own emotional pain.

Hybrid Parenting Experience

> *"I am simultaneously motivated to be with my boys but also feel burdened."*
>
> —Douglas, age 42 and six years sober before becoming a father

Some PIRs have intrinsic and extrinsic parenting traits at different times. Violet was in her early 20s when she had her first son and perceives that being young and in early recovery along with "my upbringing and the lack of emotionally healthy parents left me with dysfunctional emotional patterns, exacerbating addiction and feeling ill-equipped." She describes that after receiving trauma treatment, she has had more of an intrinsic parenting experience with her second and third children. Nancy notes that the age of her children has impacted her parenting experience. She recounts, "I felt less intuitive and less adaptable to parenting, especially when our oldest was in high school. When the kids were young, I rocked the parenting thing. I felt like I understood them, that I could meet their needs, and we had so much fun together."

For some PIRs, having the natural instinct for parenting but lacking the motivation to engage with their children can be confusing. David, who had two children before becoming sober and two afterward, has adapted quickly to some aspects of parenting but not others. He sometimes feels guilty because of his past parenting history. He admits to being "selfish with my 'self' time" while recognizing that this time is necessary for his mental health and recovery from addiction. Recovery has allowed him to keep his emotions in check because "I am slower to anger and, when confronted with my own fears, I have a process for dealing with that."

Molly Ashcroft cautions, "Both types of parents have their own set of challenges that perpetuate the relapse cycle if not addressed concurrently with alcohol and substance abuse. Parenting is a part of their identity, which is fractured when entering treatment. The shame and guilt parents hold can be immense and to break free of those bonds, it is vital to allow a safe space for them to share their most vulnerable thoughts around parenthood and the challenges they have endured."

Parent Recovery Wisdom

The following are strategies for PIRs from both PIRs and addiction treatment professionals. These ideas support extrinsic and hybrid parents who tend to have more stressors in adapting to and navigating the parenting process. Some are listed exactly as the PIRs stated to capture their tone and message. The following suggestions are meant to provide options and are not intended to be used in their entirety.

> *"I never used to share the feelings I had as an extrinsic parent with anyone, and it has been really comforting to open up (with safe people) and know I'm not alone in how I feel."*
>
> —Evelyn

For Yourself

- Remember that you can be both an extrinsic parent AND a good parent.

- Make a habit of emotionally checking in with those who may understand.
- Talk with other parents who have similar feelings.
- Take time for yourself so that you can be far more present when parenting.
- Give yourself grace and patience.
- Know that "this too shall pass" as your child(ren) grow and transition into different stages.
- Remember that perfection is the enemy of good enough and that our children need relatable role models.
- When having a hard time with the parenting role, consider outside factors such as work, health, relationships and how they may be draining you.
- Be aware of your nervous system and learn ways to self-soothe.
- Work with a therapist who specializes in parenting challenges.
- Research parenting strategies that may be the right "fit."
- Take sleep routines and scheduling seriously because they can have a detrimental impact on parenting bandwidth.
- Try to decrease commitments and unnecessary obligations, especially if parenting stress is high.
- View responsible parenting as an act of service.
- Figure out what "self-care" techniques are the most effective for you and prioritize them (see chapter 5).
- Ask for help!

With Your Child(ren)

- Recognize that what you "think" about parenting or about yourself as a parent is less important than how you act.
- Acknowledge when you have made a parenting mistake and talk about it with your child(ren).
- Find ways to bond with your baby (co-sleeping, feeding, sharing experiences).
- Dedicate time alone with each child to increase connection.
- *Show* your love.
- Increase empathy for your children by recalling how you felt when you were their age.
- Make commitments to children out loud to be held accountable.
- Give to your children what you may not have received emotionally.

- Talk with your child(ren) about why you need timeouts to de-escalate.
- Be in the moment and use parenting as a mindfulness exercise.
- Work to increase your "drive" to engage with your child(ren).

Personal Journal Entries

I have always known that parenting did not come naturally to me. I lacked the language to express precisely why or how to conceptualize it. I wondered if there was a connection with recovering from an SUD, being an only child, lacking experience with children, having an independent personality, or dealing with a combination of factors. The tension between my faint instinct and drive to push through is tangible. The concepts of intrinsic and extrinsic parents would have been illuminating during these earlier parenting years as I muddled my way through the confusion. I tried to connect with mothers in and out of recovery to see if what I was experiencing was "normal." I clung to those who seemed as lost as I was and remained in awe of those who managed motherhood with grace and ease.

November 17, 2012

Eve is 11 months old. I felt like a mother last night. For the first time, this experience did not feel surreal. Eve fell asleep cuddled on my chest, and I felt like her mother. It has taken a while for me to shift modes and identity. I still strive to feel independent while being a mother, which some view as a contradiction.

Going on a trip reined in some of my travel impulses because I've been "grounded" since being pregnant. Each weekend, I feel self-imposed pressure to take advantage of my time and to "do" things outside—and I sometimes miss the moments of simple pleasure. Eve's adorable personality has been surfacing, and I have enjoyed spending time with her.

June 17, 2013

Eve is one and a half years old. I will continue to pray for patience and sympathy when I feel reactive toward her fussiness. Today she pointed at her cheek and said "boo boo." I was able to understand that she was in pain from teething, which explained her fussy neediness.

I am not a nurturer by nature, but I will continue to work on this trait for Eve's sake.

May 9, 2014

Eve is two and a half years old. Being a mother is getting easier, but I still have "regressive" days. I am baffled by my friends who have multiple children; just thinking about that overwhelms me. I feel lucky to have made it this far—it has really pushed me in terms of my personality type, mood, patience, and ability to cope with changes.

My mind vacillates between being frustrated in the moment to appreciating the moment and feeling gratitude.

3

Family, Marriage, and Partnership

"But let there be space in your togetherness,
And let the winds of the heavens dance between you.
Love one another but make not a bond out of love:
Let it rather be a moving sea between the shores of your souls.
Fill each other's cup but drink not from one cup.
Give one another your bread but eat not from the same loaf.
Sing and dance together and be joyous, but let each one of you be alone . . ."[1]

–Kahlil Gibran

Family Systems

"FAMILY" HAS VARIOUS MEANINGS and is our initial source of attachment, nurturing, and socialization. A family system is "a household of people who not only live together but also depend on each other for basic needs and emotional support and share a common history."[2] PIRs can be part of different versions of family systems, including legal marriage, partnerships, cohabitation, divorce, separation, and friendships. Stepfamilies create new branches in a family tree.

Many have found friends to be a more reliable part of their family system than relatives. Sharon, age 53 and sober for 24 years, explains, "Since I got sober, my children have always been supported by a close group of women who are also in recovery. Their 'aunties' are solid fixtures and have always been present for us. In the Black American family, the fictive family is as valuable as and perhaps more central than the family of origin."

Developed in the 1950s by Dr. Murray Bowen, the Bowen family systems theory has been considered one of the most comprehensive views of familial behavior. It is frequently used in SUD treatment for family members and their loved ones.[3] This theory posits that healthy and problematic patterns are passed through families across generations. The therapeutic work involves the creation of genograms or a graphic of a family, with symbols and lines denoting the types of attachment, enmeshment, or strains. Some helpful concepts in family systems theory include differentiation of self and allowing family members to have separate emotions while avoiding attempts to fix others. Triangulation can lead family members to align or split apart because of a loved one's substance use. Processing these concepts as they surface can decrease anxiety, improve communication, and create healthy boundaries.[4]

The Bowen family systems theory laid the groundwork for later models, which suggest that individuals cannot be fully understood or successfully treated without first understanding how they function in the context of their family system. Through this lens, SUDs and other behavioral health issues are viewed as "an attempt to adapt to their family system so as to maintain homeostasis."[5] Similarly, family members often engage in unhealthy and sometimes surprising behaviors in response to their loved one with an SUD to maintain stability in the system. When one (or more) member of a family system has an active addiction and then becomes sober, it can cause seismic shifts. In some cases, it leads to a further fracture in the system, while in other cases, it leads to healing and unity.

Attachment theory, developed in 1958 by John Bowlby, has also been influential in treating family systems. Studies of families with SUDs show patterns that negatively impact child development, including rituals, roles, routines, communication, social life, and finances. This theory provides a route to understanding and creating quality relationships between family members and includes the idea that systems are built on the many interactions between child and parent. Healthy attachment is the "psychological immune system" that can prevent future behavioral health problems. Having parents and loved ones with SUDs can disrupt the creation of these connections and may impact future relationships.[6] PIRs who were interviewed expressed the impact that SUDs had on their families of origin, as well as the positive effects of family therapy.

Families of Origin

Family systems theories help explain the profound impact of genetics and the environment in the potential development of SUDs. However, there are additive factors, which can include impulse control issues, a history of trauma, early initial alcohol or substance use, and mental health conditions. In contrast, there are protective factors, which can include emotional resiliency, later age of initial alcohol or substance use, treatment of mental health issues, and risk-aversive tendencies. Then there is the most elusive factor of all—luck.

SUDs can often be traced to families of origin. The National Institute of Health (NIH) reports that genetics account for half the risk of developing an alcohol use disorder (AUD).[7] Environmental factors and other gene interactions influence the remainder of the risk. Familial studies indicate that environmental influences may have more of an impact on when alcohol use starts, while genetic factors impact the rate of progression to heavier use and dependency. Certain ethnic backgrounds can increase or decrease this risk.[8] For example, gene variation in those of Asian descent alters the rate of alcohol metabolism and causes negative symptoms such as flushing, nausea, and increased heart rate.[9] In some people, physical symptoms can act as protective factors to avoid developing an AUD. Epidemiologic estimates suggest that up to 29.1 percent of individuals in the United States will meet the criteria for an AUD at some point in their lifetime.[10]

Interestingly, the familial inheritance patterns for other substances vary from that of alcohol. In family studies of cannabis use disorder, a shared genetic and environmental influence throughout the stages of use was found. More specific research found that the *availability* of cannabis explained the shared environmental effect in terms of initiation and abuse. A highly genetic component of 62 percent is also correlated with when use starts. Research has found that the heritability of opiate use disorder is 50 percent for individuals using *any* substances and 38 percent for opioid use specifically. Interestingly, there is little evidence of cocaine-specific genetic influences, but there is evidence of 40 percent–80 percent shared genetic vulnerability when cocaine use is combined with other substances, specifically cannabis.[11]

Sadly, it is estimated that more than 8 million children and adolescents live with at least one parent who has an active SUD—amounting to 1 in 10 of the population younger than 18.[12] After hearing the childhood experiences of many PIRs, these statistics may even be low. Almost all PIRs interviewed came from families with one or more parents who had an SUD. In contrast, the control group of parents not in recovery interviewed reported that 50 percent had SUD in their family, 39.3 percent did not, and 10.7 percent were not sure. Chris, sober 16 years and married to a PIR, reports that "Both of our families have histories of SUDs, mental health, and trauma. These have shown themselves throughout our lives and journeys." Laura, sober for 38 years and also married to a PIR, adds that some members of her family drink socially, others drink to excess, and still others are in recovery. Some individuals with SUDs in their family history choose not to use substances themselves, but the next generation has a different experience. Will, age 63 and married to a PIR, notes that his grandfather was an alcoholic and a maternal uncle died from alcoholism, but neither of his parents drank often. Natasha, sober for six years, and an adult child of parents with SUDs is aware that she has broken the cycle in her family and expresses that it can feel "Unnatural to be sober because my destiny was to die of this disease."

Evelyn, age 39, was adopted into a family with no substance issues. The power of the genetic component was evident when she recently learned the identity of her biological father and that alcoholism ran in his family. She explains, "This was oddly comforting to me, as the lack of understanding about addiction in my adoptive family only made me feel the 'you're different from everyone else' even more." SUDs can also develop without a genetic history. Steve, sober for 16 years, is one of the only PIRs interviewed who did not have a family history and notes, "I am the black sheep of my family, and no one is an alcoholic."

Most PIRs are deeply aware of the role of genetics and the chances that their children may develop an SUD. (For more on this, as well as how and when PIRs choose to talk about addiction with their children, see chapter 8.)

Family Support

Having a child is a one-of-a-kind experience that can be both a blessing and a stressor for marriages and partnerships. Research on the impact of having a newborn on marital satisfaction found that 90 percent of couples experienced a small to medium negative effect.[13] In one study, 25 percent of couples were "in some distress" by the time their child was 18 months old.[14] Once a child enters the picture, all areas of life and partnerships experience notable shifts—a true test of the relationship's stability. Recovery is the foundation of PIRs' relationships, and if built on an unstable footing, the entire family system can be impacted.

PIRs in long-term recovery report being in marriages or partnerships with either an individual in recovery or someone who has an awareness and sensitivity around substance use. There can be many benefits to partnering with someone in recovery. But there may also be competing needs or an unhealthy attachment to their partner's recovery status. The need to accommodate both partners' recovery can lead to a deviation in traditional gender roles and a need for flexibility within the couple's household and childcare responsibilities. Cassie, sober for 15 years, notes, "Thankfully, both my husband and I have been sober since becoming parents, but we have had to adjust our recovery to fit our family life. Balancing busy schedules and work can be challenging." She also expresses the importance of their continued recovery growth as a couple, stating, "It is very important that my partner and I are engaging in activities that aid our recovery. When I am not, my life becomes challenging and unmanageable." Jackie, sober for 14 years and married to a PIR adds, "The strength and quality of our individual programs of recovery impact the family system. We are not always in the same place with our spiritual condition or ability to utilize the tools of recovery." She also emphasizes that she and her partner have not relied solely on each other for recovery support and that "this separation has been helpful in navigating different levels of healing that arise during the recovery process." David, sober for 19 years and married to a PIR, compares his marriage to a building foundation in that, "when one support column is impacted, the entire system is impacted. I try not to take it on, but what my spouse goes through, I go through and vice versa." Valerie, sober for 24 years and also married to a PIR, emphasizes that each partner needs to continue working on their recovery long after the more difficult early years and that "even years later, my recovery is a top priority."

Having a partner in recovery can be helpful but is not necessary. PIRs with partners not in recovery emphasized the significance of their loved one's healthy relationship with alcohol or substances. PIRs also described the need for their partners to support them and limit their substance use. Joan, sober for 10 years and married to an individual not in recovery, comments that her family "makes sure my drink of choice (seltzer) is available. They are conscious of how much they drink around me, and some do not drink around me." Natasha is married to a husband who drinks alcohol and reports that he drinks less now that she is sober. Still, she emphasizes, "I have to put my recovery above everything else, and I also separate it from my family system and its wellness." Stacie, 11 years sober with a husband who drinks moderately, admits that "sometimes my husband's drinking bothers me, but I think that is more of a control issue for me than a recovery issue." She recommends "Focusing on what you have control over—yourself. I had to believe in myself before my family system would."

Some spouses choose not to drink for other reasons, such as indifference or troubling family histories. Jake, sober for 12 years, said his wife has decided not to drink to respect his recovery. Rebecca, sober for two years, has a husband who grew up in an alcoholic home and, as a result, he has never had a drink or used a substance.

PIRs who get sober while in a relationship with someone who has an active SUD or who lacks respect for their recovery have a higher chance of relapse or breaking up. Tracie, sober for two years, reveals, "My husband moved out within 60 days of my sobriety and hasn't been back. We are now divorced. He was not able to be emotionally or physically supportive of me or our daughters when I got sober." Evelyn recalls that her first husband was not compassionate but instead would be "hypercritical and use humor to shame me in a toxic way." She has since divorced and is in a long-term relationship with another sober individual. Will's first spouse was not in recovery, and now he is married to a PIR. He points out that his current wife "understands my alcoholism—she just gets it. She comes to meetings with me, and this has been the easy way compared with being married to someone who had been jealous of my recovery fellowship and questioned why I needed to go to meetings."

The need for PIRs to prioritize their recovery above the needs of their children is counter to the message many parents are raised to believe. However, if they do not have a charged battery, they have nothing to give. Plus, they risk their emotional and physical sobriety. Valerie says, "When we are not taking care of ourselves and asking one another for help, we can get resentful. So, while it is difficult to juggle kids and recovery, we make it a point to." Nancy, sober for 31 years and married to a PIR, expresses that the gains of supporting her wife outweigh the burden, stating, "It wasn't always easy to take care of two young children by myself while my wife was at a recovery meeting, but it was worth it. Staying connected to other parents in my 12-step group has been a lifesaver." Steve cautions, "If we sacrifice our needs so much for our son's needs, we could lose ourselves and become miserable—this doesn't mean that he is not important or that we do not love him."

Dating can pose challenges for PIRs and elicit different preferences. Some limit themselves to dating only those who are in recovery or abstinent, while others do not. Sharon, sober for 24 years, discloses, "I have avoided having long-term relationships with men who use substances because I would rather be alone. My most recent partner drank socially without any flags, so I felt safe in that situation." Chris, sober for 17 years, doesn't have a preference if whom he is dating is sober or not—but his deal breaker is if the person is using any substance in excess. His most recent girlfriend used marijuana, but he reported that it did not interfere with her productivity or organization, and he remained comfortable with this. Most important when dating is that PIRs are honest with themselves and others about their personal needs and limits.

Family Treatment

Addiction *is* a family disease. All family members are affected—causing shifts in behaviors, relationships, physical condition, and emotional health. The genetic component also increases the chances that other biological family members will have SUDs. The most promising long-term treatment outcomes are in families in which all immediate family members seek help and engage in their own recovery processes.[15] Research shows that family therapy can decrease substance misuse for other adolescent family members[16] and children affected by parental

SUDs.[17] Therapy and coaching can provide a neutral space for family members and loved ones to process the impact on them as well as to understand multiple family perspectives. Liz Modugno, LCSW, LADC, and Owner of Aspire Counseling of CT, conceptualizes how addiction and recovery impact a family with the metaphor of a hanging planet mobile. She elaborates,

> Whenever you touch, add, remove, or change the position of the planets on the mobile, it would sway and tilt, but eventually it would find balance again and stop. Family members are much like the planets that have swayed and moved throughout time. When new behaviors form, the position or weight of the parts shift until balance is achieved, sometimes healthy and sometimes unhealthy. . . . A couple's therapist, family therapist or individual therapist can help family members recognize these changes, process emotions and feelings, and move toward a healthy and balanced family dynamic.

Discussing families and addiction is hard to do without mentioning the concept of codependency. Melody Beattie's book *Codependent No More* is a staple in the family therapy world. The codependent person can be defined as "one who has let another person's behavior affect him or her and who is obsessed with controlling that person's behavior."[18] This term has gained a negative connotation over time and may be replaced with descriptors such as: enmeshed, attached, overinvolved, entangled, and anchored. Detachment is another related critical concept that continues to have clinical relevance; it is based on the premise of "mentally, emotionally, and physically disengaging ourselves from unhealthy (and frequently painful) entanglement with another person's life and responsibilities, and from problems we cannot solve."[19] While this interpersonal strategy can be directed to any relationship that warrants it, most apply it to the loved ones of those with addiction and mental health conditions. The description and interpretation of detachment can sound cold and callous; however, "It is not detaching from the person whom we care about, but from the agony of involvement."[20]

The Community Reinforcement and Family Training (CRAFT) therapeutic model has offered evidence-based strategies for families in group and individual settings since the early 2000s. This approach is based on the idea that family members can make sobriety seem more attractive to their loved one, but does not initially recommend detachment unless for safety reasons. The core text *Get Your Loved One Sober: Alternatives to Nagging, Pleading, and Threatening* by Robert Meyers and Brenda Wolfe guides family members in appropriate and strategic engagement intended to make the relationships work before and after their loved one has gotten sober.[21] Dan Griffin, author of several books including *Amazing Dads! Fatherhood Curriculum* and owner of Griffin Recovery Enterprises, and his wife Nancy Griffin discuss the concept of family recovery. Dan explains that he was sober when they met, and Nancy had no experience with the process of recovery. She recalls that she had "a pretty one-dimensional understanding of what an alcoholic is, but now I have this very comprehensive understanding of recovery. It's the dynamics of interpersonal relationships. It's the family system." Nancy adds, "It is very important to have a program of recovery for the entire family. There's no way to take away your recovery and separate it from the recovery of the family." She highlights the power of being exposed to the recovery lifestyle and that "the framework that recovery brings, the dimensions it brings to your relationships, and the ability to apply it and use it in all areas of your life, including parenting, is great. It is profound."[22]

Almost all PIRs interviewed were fortunate to have family members who supported their recovery and whom they relied on in many ways. However, in some situations, PIRs need to set boundaries with friends or family. Diana Clark, JD, MA in her *Family Healing Strategies* workbook defines boundaries as "Mechanisms that bring safety into your life by establishing control. They act as limits for what you will do as well as what you will and will not permit others to do."[23] Healthy boundaries can include staying focused on your growth and recovery, determining and maintaining your own values and opinions regardless of what someone else wants, respect for others and yourself, and trusting your own intuition and decisions. In contrast, unhealthy boundaries can include oversharing when first meeting someone, trusting everyone or no one, giving someone else power over your decisions and putting other's needs before your recovery and wellness.[24] Specific examples of setting boundaries are declining an invitation to a holiday event because there will be excessive drinking, limiting interactions with friends or family who create emotionally charged conversations, not inviting friends or family into the home who do not respect recovery or rules set around substance use, and an individual telling a loved one they are not willing to spend time with them unless they are sober.

PIRs in a relationship with another person in recovery may benefit from being mindful of their boundaries around their level of attachment to their partner's recovery. While it is human nature to have some level of attachment to a loved one's wellness and safety, reliance on another's stability for one's own can be detrimental. The PIRs interviewed clarified that a level of detachment from their partner's behaviors and emotions is vital to a healthy relationship. Some PIRs have addressed issues of attachment and detachment in their therapeutic work. Chase, sober 17 years and single, has been in relationships with partners who were both in and not in recovery. He reports that this has not significantly affected his recovery. While his level of autonomy is not the norm, it is still possible. Alex emphasizes that PIRs need to base their wellness on themselves and not on how their loved one is doing. He adds that taking care of yourself is accepting that you have "zero control" over your loved one. This concept of emotional detachment is the underpinning of many support groups for the loved ones of those with SUDs.

Social and family support for PIRs is instrumental in relapse prevention. Family and loved ones' behaviors can foster a positive environment for their loved ones, including being honest, supporting treatment, providing emotional strength, and showing consistency. In contrast, family traits that may increase the risk of relapse are lacking knowledge about SUDs, not showing recovery support, demonstrating unhealthy boundaries, having severe family systems issues, and actively using substances.[25] Jennifer Barba, LCSW, Founder and CEO of the CT Healing Center and Keystone House Recovery Homes has found, "One remarkable distinction lies in the vital support and accountability that families provide when they actively participate in the recovery journey. I've seen firsthand how a strong support network can work wonders, offering unwavering understanding, encouragement, and motivation to loved ones in recovery. It's incredible how this kind of support boosts their confidence, fuels their commitment to change, and ultimately enhances their chances of long-term sobriety."

Many individuals with long-term recovery report that their family system was able to adapt and grow along with them. The treatment focus is often on the family member with the SUD, which can dilute the treatment offered to or attended by loved ones and lower their chances of recovery. Research and experts concur about the importance of appropriate family involvement in this healing process. Molly Ashcroft,

CADC, ICADC, emphasizes the importance of family therapy, coaching, and overall change. "Family members are still under the impression that if their loved one gets well and remains sober, then the family system will be repaired. What loved ones don't realize is that the fracture within the family system is usually much larger than one family member's addiction. Each family member has been curated for their role in the system and is not even aware of it." Susan Berlin, LICSW, CASAC, ICADC, therapist, and CCO of Verve Behavioral Health has observed that "The parent *not* in recovery also has challenges for self-care and has a lot to work through. They may really want the PIR to do more now that they are sober and it is a very hard balance for both parents to figure out." She adds that family members of PIRs can sometimes have mental health and "addictive" behaviors that go untreated because "they have been dealing with so much in the face of their partner's addiction—all they want is for their partner to stop using so that life can be 'normal.'" She recommends couples therapy with an addiction specialist to address these family dynamics. Jill Griffin, LADC, LCSW, finds that the recovery process is often just as hard for loved ones because they may not understand the timeline, necessary boundaries, or have realistic expectations. Sheila Coleman, DSW, LMSW, suggests that family members get help simultaneously so that they can "heal together."

Evelyn explains that her family system's wellness positively impacted her because "everyone learned to put their own oxygen mask on first." She contrasts this to how they behaved in the past, stating, "When I was drinking, it was always about 'how to fix Evelyn,' and that made my shame and thus my drinking worse." Joan has observed that while others in her family do not have an SUD, they have recognized and addressed their own wellness in terms of psychological, social, and physical needs. She found it helpful that, initially, her husband attended therapy and 12-step meetings with her while others learned about addiction and how best to support her.

Loved ones often need help coping with the impact of a PIR's substance use. Liz Modugno reported that "A common pattern I see in therapy is that spouses and family members learn ways to survive while their loved one is in active addiction. For example, sometimes a spouse will form an entire life outside of the relationship with the identified patient, often committing to work, family or other obligations to distract themselves and become independent from that partner. Once their partner enters into recovery, many healthy dynamics need to be relearned by both parties." Steve explains that his sister went to therapy and that he is "proud of her for doing that work. She has struggled and asked for help, and it has been good for our relationship as she was traumatized by my use." Sharon expresses that many of her family members have long-term sobriety and that their wellness "fortifies me." Stacie states that her husband has attended several Al-Anon meetings and marriage counseling because he "Would not talk about any issues or feelings, so he has made a ton of progress that has absolutely helped me in my recovery." Additionally, she used to find her mother "very controlling, but she has worked hard to trust me more and to be more careful with her wording of things—making suggestions instead of demands."

While the focus can often be on the impact of a partner's support, children can also play a crucial role. Tracie's 11 and 13-year-old daughters "were overjoyed when I got sober and participated in my recovery from the beginning—asking questions about my meetings, celebrating milestones with me, and getting to know my new friends in recovery." Her daughters have both enjoyed and benefited from therapy because "it's helping them adjust to the changes in our family dynamic and to heal from years of damage my drinking caused." She strongly feels their support and belief in her ability to stay sober have helped her through her darkest days.

PIRs' initial sobriety shifted the homeostasis in some family systems, leading to unexpected changes. Mason, sober for 19 years and married to a PIR, points out that his father and brother became sober after his recovery. He and his wife have also attended years of therapy, and "the healthier and more aware each member of the family is, the more peaceful and fulfilling day-to-day life becomes." Alex, sober for 12 years and married to another PIR, describes that after he became sober, his "father started to fall apart, my sister didn't address her trauma from the past, and roles began to reverse." He was fortunate that they both reached out to him for help, which has also strengthened their bond.

Home Environment

Home should be a sanctuary, a space where PIRs can have some control over the substances, the behaviors, and the company that they keep.

PIRs have differing family systems which can include partners who do drink or use substances, while other couples are both sober and still others are single. Therefore, the responses varied on whether PIRs are comfortable having alcohol or substances in their home, but demonstrate the importance of individuals at all stages of recovery determining their own parameters and communicating their needs to those around them. When asked if they allow alcohol or substances in their home, PIRs offered their personal experience protecting their environment in a world where others drink or use substances.

- "No, I don't. When I got sober, my husband at the time was a social drinker and he agreed not to have alcohol in the house. I find that, even now, if there is alcohol in the house, I am hyper-aware of it, even if I don't want to drink it. If someone doesn't know I am sober and brings alcohol over, I ask them to take it home with them." —Evelyn
- "No, I don't allow it for myself *and* my teenagers. It gave them comfort knowing it wasn't around anymore and if people can't come over to my house for dinner or a BBQ and not drink, then they simply shouldn't come. Hard boundary for me and my girls." —Tracie
- "I do. And I don't want to make it a thing by asking other people not to drink, but it doesn't bother me. Right now, there is a bottle of wine in my fridge left over from a women's party I had over the summer. I like watching people relax and have a glass of wine and I am perfectly happy having iced tea or water. I think it's because alcohol wasn't my drug of choice and because I've been in recovery for so many years." —Cathy, sober 23 years
- "No. I like the lifestyle of a substance-free environment." —David
- "Yes. I have a spouse who doesn't have a problem. The alcohol is kept out of sight." —Joan
- "I do. I have other adults living in my house, we have a few rules. I don't put booze out or away. I don't want you 'drunk' in my house. My kids respect my sobriety enough to drink only at home on holidays and then a glass or two of wine." —Laura
- "I don't keep alcohol in the house because I don't drink it. If others come to my house for dinner, I don't provide it, but I will advise guests to feel free to bring some wine if they would like. I do not feel that it is necessary to restrict others." —Marilyn

- "There is alcohol because my husband drinks, but never a surplus." —Natasha
- "No. I don't allow alcohol or any addictive substances in my home. I protect my sobriety at all costs." —Rebecca
- "My husband drinks, but the only alcohol he brings into the house is beer. I don't like having wine or hard alcohol in the house because that is what I enjoyed drinking. He will only buy a six-pack and that helps to keep me accountable because I know he would notice if one went missing." —Stacie
- "I allow friends and family to bring their own alcohol over if they choose, but we do not keep alcohol in the home for people." —Jackie

Parent Recovery Wisdom

"The best thing I ever read was an article about a mother with healthy and successful daughters. She said the secret to parenting is for 'my husband and I to take care of ourselves; then they will be happy.' This was different than what I had learned—that being a parent is all about putting yourself last and the child first."

—Steve

Both PIRs and addiction treatment professionals highlight the following strategies and ideas for couples, immediate family members, and extended family members to engage in ongoing growth, wellness, and healing. Some of these are listed exactly as stated by the PIRs to capture their precise message. The following suggestions are meant to provide options and are not intended to be used in their entirety.

For Couples and Household Members

- Foster a dynamic of open, honest, and non-judgmental communication.
- Engage in wellness activities as a couple and family.
- Discuss what life in recovery may look like or household changes that should happen.

- Find childcare for "date nights" and "remember why we were together outside of having children."
- Ask for what you really need and try not to operate from a place of shame and guilt.
- Attend family or couples counseling/coaching with an addiction specialist.
- Recognize that early sobriety requires more time and effort than later "maintenance" phases, for both you or your partner.
- Create open lines of communication for both partners to identify their needs and concerns.
- Respect that one person may need more "downtime" than the other.
- Have a shared calendar to stay organized and schedule wellness timeslots.
- Allow each partner to have a night off and engage in activities that can recharge.
- Remember that your individual drive for transformation can inspire family members.

For Partners

- Join self-help meetings for loved ones of those with SUDs (i.e., Al-Anon, Nar-Anon, SHE RECOVERS, Learn 2 Cope, and more) (see Resources section).
- Give your partner the space to prioritize their recovery and wellness even if you feel lonely or jealous of their activities and supports.
- Utilize a shared calendar for scheduling self-care and recovery-related activities for both partners.
- There is no going back to the "old normal" and only "What do you want to build going forward?"
- Avoid the "tally rabbit hole" of comparing each other's alone or wellness time.
- Be mindful of your substance use and do not have substances in the home for at least the first 90 days.
- Be aware of your own needs and limitations.
- Be aware of when your partner or loved one appears in distress, "drowning," or burnt out from parenting and offer to step up.
- Ask how you can be of support instead of guessing.

For PIRs

- Avoid overreliance on your partner for help; seek outside peers and resources.
- Talk with your partner about various aspects of parenting and recovery before having children (discipline, co-sleeping, schedules, self-care, plan for relapse, etc.).
- Share your relapse prevention plan so that your partner can be informed.
- Ask your partner or co-parent for help and "tap out" or delegate when needed or possible.
- When stable, ask how you can increase your efforts as a parent and partner.
- Communicate about the weekly schedule, including self-care/recovery time.

For Engaging with Extended Family

- Ask available family members for childcare support to allow for self-care or recovery-related activities.
- Connect with other families (related or not) who are engaging in wellness-focused lifestyles.
- Be honest about your needs.
- Set necessary boundaries around loved ones and family drinking and using substances in your presence—including not attending events.
- Encourage engagement in family education about addiction, therapy, or other recovery-based groups for their healing process.
- Expect that some family members will not engage in help, believing that it is "not their problem."
- Provide family support resources and book recommendations.
- Expect that the pace of your loved ones' recovery process may differ from yours.
- Take the necessary time to heal before re-engaging fully with some relationships.
- Establish boundaries as needed and in a loving way.

Personal Journal Entries

Motherhood has been a journey I could never have fully prepared for personally or within my marriage. I am fortunate to have married a man in recovery who has intrinsic parenting qualities that complement my more extrinsic ones. We also understand and respect each other's needs and parenting "time outs." While parenting adds a new layer of responsibility, it has been imperative to balance that with wellness activities.

August 20, 2011—*Pregnant*

Josh has been amazing and more supportive than I could have ever imagined. I feel so close to him and blessed to have him as my husband. I love him deeper each day.

Everyone has stress and fear in their lives in different ways. No one is exempt. I pray to grow stronger through this experience and know that God has a plan for me. It seems this is "mommy boot camp" as these tests are going to help me to cope with the inevitable uncertainty of motherhood.

July 7, 2013—*Eve, 1.5 years old*

Gratitude: Peace in my life, friends, sober community, Eve's laughter and playing at the beach.

Learning new activities, health/mental health, blessed that Josh and I have the same goals in life, lifestyle choice, and rhythm.

July 20, 2013

I want to work on being more sensitive to Josh's emotions and needs as he has always been for me. I still cannot believe how level my mood has felt, and I am so grateful each day and each night when I go to sleep. Thankful for the life that Josh and I have created—safe, healthy, secure.

July 22, 2013

I had little patience with Eve last night and just needed time to "veg out." The constancy of the relationship can feel overwhelming. I did ask for support from Josh.

July 23, 2013

Gratitude: sober network, boundaries, stability, Eve's energy and laying on my lap, time to recharge.

September 28, 2013

At Kripalu retreat: The Buddhist book *When Things Fall Apart* is resonating with me as it encourages us to sink into the discomfort—when I want to run away from some of it. I also rely on Josh for comfort but have been finding my own way.

The energy balancing session I had was powerful in effect but without the intrusion of acupuncture or massage—pure energy from another person. I also hope to be able to shift my own energy through yoga and stretching movements at home. I am realizing the power of energy released through my body.

4

Get a Life

Finding a Personal and Professional Identity

"The greatest challenge of becoming a parent has been maintaining an identity of my own while being a present and attentive parent."

—Evelyn

"GETTING A LIFE" MEANS different things to different parents. For some, having a child(ren) fulfills their deepest desires and sense of purpose. Other mothers and fathers maintain a desire and need to also pursue academic or career goals. Still others integrate volunteering, community service, or hobbies into their parenting role.

Parental roles have evolved and are impacted by many factors, including culture, gender, sexual identity, marital status, race, religion, age, education, financial situation, and family history. Traditional male and female roles have likely been the most impacted by the increase in women attaining higher education and entering the labor force over the second half of the twentieth century—specifically from the 1960s through the 1980s. Following the women's rights movement era, from 1970 to 2021, the proportion of women who pursued a college degree quadrupled while it doubled for men. In 2020, 57 percent of women worked full-time compared with just 40.7 percent in 1970.[1]

Marital status has a significant impact on work patterns as well. In 2021, never-married women had the highest work engagement at 64.3 percent, separated women at 62.4 percent, divorced women at 59 percent, and married women at 56.9 percent. In comparison and regardless of marital status, men are more likely to be employed, with rates of 70.9 percent for married men and 71.3 percent for separated men. Men were the sole providers in just 17 percent of married opposite-sex couples in 2020 versus 35.6 percent in 1967.[2]

Having younger children notably decreased women's engagement in the labor force but has been less so for men. Mothers with children six to 17 years old were working at a rate of 75.8 percent compared with 66.5 percent for mothers with children younger than six and an even lower percentage for mothers (64.5%) with children younger than three. Fathers, in contrast, averaged 93 percent employment regardless of the age of their children under 18.[3]

While these statistics represent general trends, couples may follow more or less traditional parenting and work roles. Many women (and some men) have chosen or have defaulted into stay-at-home roles within their families. For example, some men have taken on more of the caregiving role, while their partner has become the financial provider. Some single parents take on dual roles as caregiver and financial provider, while differing custody arrangements can allow for some flexibility.

An important point is that educational and socioeconomic standing can determine the ability to *choose* employment status. In many families, both partners or single parents are obligated to work—it is not a matter of preference. Other families like to have two incomes to support their lifestyle, although they could manage on one. Parenting generally comes with an increase in financial responsibility, leading some to feel stuck in their current job, even if it is not ideal for their recovery. In a post-pandemic world, the work landscape has shifted to offer many more remote job options, providing more flexibility with time and logistics.

Men's parental roles have also evolved. Many men are now expected to be more "hands-on" and may find themselves juggling work and parental obligations. While blurring these roles has afforded more flexibility, it can also lead to confusion around work and the delegation of household and parental tasks.

Personal and Professional Identity

Personal identity can be defined as "the distinguishing character or personality of an individual **or** the relation established by psychological identification."[4] Innumerable factors impact our identity, as well as situation-based labels that are subscribed to, including "mother," "father," "in recovery," "working," "stay-at-home," and so on. Additionally, individuals consciously or subconsciously label themselves with other identity descriptors, such as independent, caring, nurturing, humorous, adventurous, rebellious, carefree, rigid, and others.

"Identity" considered through the lens of parenting is not often discussed or written about. However, it is a noteworthy aspect of the adjustment to becoming a mother or father. Many parents-to-be spend countless hours obtaining knowledge and the "stuff" they will need. Nurseries are meticulously decorated as the nesting instinct kicks in. Parents receive gifts at baby showers that prepare for every possible baby need. Many parents-to-be saturate themselves by absorbing books, websites, podcasts, and articles in an effort to ready themselves for the new arrival. But there is not enough information or baby supplies in the world to adequately plan for the earth-shattering life and identity shifts that a newborn brings.

New parents often talk about the challenges, including interrupted sleep, disrupted routines, and overwhelming emotions. While they may be ready materially and intellectually, planning for the psychological and emotional changes is impossible. Parenting books frequently focus on the best strategies for raising children, but a gap remains—the literature does not discuss the existential impact on parents or provide insight into or knowledge of the personal and professional identity shifts that are likely to occur. These changes can be most profound for the parent who takes a leave from work or handles most of the initial childcare responsibilities. Jessica Valenti, in her book, *Why Have Kids: A New Mother Explores the Truth About Parenting and Happiness*, interviewed mothers in a raw and honest way and found that "The overwhelming sentiment, however, was the feeling of loss of self, the terrifying reality that their lives had been subsumed into the needs of their child. . . . Everything that made us an individual that made us unique, no longer matters. It's our role as a mother that defines us."[5] Rachel Brownell, PIR and author of *Mommy Doesn't Drink Here Anymore*, elaborates, "The transition to parenthood—the letting go of self, the deep responsibility for another human being, the occasional despair when encountering the tectonic shifts parenting requires—amplifies the best and the worse in each of us. For those with potential drug or alcohol problems, these challenges are compounded by fuzzy things, addiction, and an obsession with obliterating reality."[6]

When getting sober, PIRs spend a significant amount of time reframing their identity from an individual with an active SUD to a person in recovery. The scars of past substance use never completely fade, but recovery involves a transformation in self-perception. (For a discussion of the lifestyle changes necessary to maintain long-term recovery, see chapter 1.) Jill Griffin, LCSW, LADC, emphasizes the importance of this sense of connection with self, "Sobriety means discovering who you really are because drugs and alcohol numb us from feeling and experiencing our true selves."

For many PIRs, having a child(ren) adds to their positive sense of self and allows them to move past the negative self-perception they had in active addiction. Claire, an occupational therapist for children, became sober when her first son was six months old and recalls,

> Personally, at that time, I felt a lot of shame and self-doubt, but professionally, I still maintained a higher regard for myself as "Claire, the occupational therapist." I leaned into my career and motherhood, and I felt like it gave me a sense of purpose, a role that brought me dignity and self-worth. Being a mother not only gave me a new role and identity, one that I desperately needed in those early days of sobriety but also motivation to stay sober, work on my emotional sobriety and be as conscious of a parent as I could be.

Mason, an EMT and father of three, has been "Finding greater purpose and fulfillment" since becoming a father. Natasha, a lawyer and mother of a newborn, has felt empowered: "I realize that I can do anything sober, and I feel like I have the greatest reason to stay sober now. It is also the test and demonstrates the strength of my sobriety because parenting helps me to let go of control and also to want to continue to work through the causes and conditions of my drinking and childhood traumas." Jake, a business owner and father of a young girl, expresses, "Being a parent created the largest shift in my life. The connection between my daughter, my wife and me is overwhelming. It's hard to explain how I changed, but I became a man. Many new experiences had new meaning."

Parenthood can also help PIRs commit to a professional path that may not have been a priority before. Violet, a marketing manager and mother of three, elaborates, "My professional identity went from non-existent to a level of heavy responsibility. Prior to having my first child, I bounced around quite a bit. I quit jobs the moment I felt like it and had no fear about doing so. After having my first child, I felt a strong urge and responsibility to change my ways. After staying home for three months, I sought a full-time job and never looked back." She realized that her family needed her to be consistent at work—to provide what she had not received as a child. Kevin, age 51, was a corrections officer for many years and "all I had to worry about before parenthood was myself and maybe the impact on my wife if something bad happened." He began to recognize the substance use, mental health, and marital toll that this job had on other officers. He explained that "Substance use was not only common but socially acceptable and encouraged. The divorce rate among officers was very high, and we had a suicide rate nine times higher than non-first responders. Not only were staff suffering, but the cumulative trauma that transferred to our loved ones was bothersome to me." He chose to move on to a career as an SUD treatment marketing manager for the sake of his recovery, his wife, and his daughter. Kevin allowed his professional identity to shift to a lower-intensity career but one that he finds fulfilling.

Maintaining a clear sense of grounding can become difficult with the immense shifts parenthood brings. Rachel Brownell captures this evolution, "Since becoming a mother five years before, I've longed to hang on to a part of myself that isn't smeared in Mommy goo. The part that laughs at parties, looks good in heels, and earns a living while spending quality time with loved ones. I want to be the anti-June Cleaver, the un-wife, the un-mother, loving and present, but not invisible or brainless."[7] Cassie, a pharmaceutical researcher with a young son, adds,

> It was really hard. I had an idea of my career path and loved my job. Adding in being a parent on top of career and self-help meetings sometimes made it feel impossible. I felt selfish when I became a mom and wanted my old life back. When I became a parent, I felt that I lost my identity that I had found getting sober, and I still struggle with that today. It does not help that I took on the main parental role. I still miss the person I was before I became a parent.

Violet recalls, "Since becoming a parent, there have been points in my life where I have felt like I have lost my identity. Yet, I have also struggled with guilt in the past when leaving my children to take time out for myself." Natasha found that a work promotion as a new mother helped her feel more like herself, increased her confidence, and reminded her to maintain balance.

Parental identity develops with more time to acclimate to the role and with growth of the child(ren). Nancy, a teacher with two older children, describes,

> Parenthood turned my personal identity upside down. I was now a parent, holy wow! Everything became about the baby, and then the babies and then the kids. And even though they are now in their 20s, they are still "the kids." Bigger kids, bigger problems. As they grew, though, my wife and I became very well aware that our entire lives could be swallowed up by being parents. We worked hard to continue to develop other parts of our identity. It isn't a coincidence that I became a big hiker and outdoor enthusiast when the kids became teenagers. It is now a big part of my identity.

She has grown spiritually from having a part of her life exist where the focus was not solely on being a parent but also on her connection with another community.

Parenting and Recovery Identity

There is an undeniable impact on the relationship between becoming a parent and being in recovery. Parents must adjust to this new life, new schedule, and new role. Before becoming a parent, many rely on their identity as a "person in recovery" and the associated lifestyle. When parenting is added to the equation, reactions differ. Molly Ashcroft, CADC, ICADC, has observed that PIRs in treatment routinely put their children before their recovery. She notes that this is both a threat to their current sobriety and can leave them vulnerable to relapse when the child becomes older and less dependent. Jennifer Barba, LCSW, has observed that the greatest identity challenge is in "navigating the shift in priorities and adjusting routines to accommodate parenting responsibilities while maintaining sobriety. They must reconcile their past actions and behavior with their new role as a parent—integrating their recovery identity with their identity as a caregiver."

Some PIRs reported that becoming a parent solidified their commitment toward recovery because of the immense responsibility it entails, the selflessness it requires, and the desire to give a better life to their children. Jackie states, "Becoming a parent has forced me to reprioritize my life while keeping recovery in the forefront because my belief is that without my sobriety, I cannot be an effective partner or parent." Cathy, a writer, added, "My son became my reason for living my best life possible in all ways. Not only did I get more serious about my sobriety, I also went back to school, earned my master's degree and finally became a working writer and teacher, something I had wanted to do for 30 years. . . . It just came about because I was a single mother determined to be a better parent to him than my parents were to me." Mason affirms, "My commitment to 'not using, no matter what' was fortified with the responsibility of this little human in my care."

Moving into the early parenthood phase of life can lead those in recovery to stray from the clinical and self-help supports they once relied on. This can be an extremely disorienting and vulnerable time for PIRs. Before becoming a parent, it may have been easier to prioritize and commit to recovery activities. But after becoming a parent, PIRs face competing obligations and can experience "recovery guilt" from time to time. The cautionary expression, "Whatever you put in front of your recovery, you could lose," often sticks in the back of the mind of many PIRs. Nicole Castiglioni, LPC, a therapist in private practice, observed,

> Parenting, especially during the early stages, can be incredibly isolating. While this can be difficult for any parent, we know this can be detrimental for a parent in recovery. I have sat with so many parents in recovery who were clearly committed to their recovery and strongly motivated for continued healing and change but struggled significantly to stay connected to recovery supports (attendance at 12-step meetings, other support groups, therapy, etc.). They also may need to navigate other barriers, such as finding reliable childcare, having limited financial resources or simply being purely exhausted at times due to the demands of caring for a child in addition to other responsibilities.

She adds that the disconnection PIRs may face can pull them further away from relationships and activities that were part of their identity. Cassie illustrates, "When becoming a parent, at first, I was not able to attend as many meetings or be engaged with recovery the way I had before.

I remember hearing a meeting speaker say that once women get married and have kids, they stop going to meetings. This intrigued me, and while I never stopped going to meetings, I did attend fewer. . . . I would also say there were positive aspects, mostly challenging me to learn about myself and what I liked as a person." Steve, a business owner and father of a newborn, notes confusion in that, "It has been difficult to choose between putting my son to bed and going to a meeting and how much time for self-wellness versus how much for him? I want to be a good partner and carry my weight in my marriage, but I wrestle with how to balance her self-care needs as well." Liz Modugno, LCSW, LADC, has encouraged clients struggling with this type of guilt to reframe their thoughts from "meetings and therapy take away from my kids and family" to "meetings and therapy give me and my children a sober and healthy life together." She also suggests playing the tape forward and exploring what would really happen if they did not put their sobriety first. Nancy Nitenson, MD, is board-certified in addiction psychiatry and both prescribes and conducts therapy for her clients. She has found that the greatest challenge of PIRs "solidly rooted" in their recovery is drifting away from their treatment plan. She suggests "to always have some recovery ritual, it might be their favorite weekly self-help meeting or possibly a session with an addiction professional—even meeting biweekly or monthly to focus on life issues, such as work and family, while always keeping an eye on recovery, can be especially helpful for parents."

For other PIRs, becoming sober after becoming a parent may begin with feelings of shame but then develop into newfound confidence. Liz Modugno reflects,

> One of the greatest identity challenges for PIRs that have become sober *after* becoming parents is the shame and guilt of who they used to be as a person during active addiction. They may have missed out on parts of their children's lives or had unhealthy relationships with their children during active addiction. They can find it hard to put themselves first in recovery, prioritize their recovery, take time to attend meetings, take time for therapy sessions, take time to check into rehab or complete a therapeutic program. I strongly emphasize that without sobriety, there is no healthy life with their children and families.

Nicole Castiglioni also notes that these PIRs often feel guilty for leaving their child when they "don't have to" for recovery or self-care–related activities and question if they are deserving or worthy of taking that time for themselves. However, she finds that "Many other identity-related challenges stem from this. Maintaining a connection to recovery supports and reducing isolation is critical to trying to navigate other areas of their life and recovery journey." Dr. Nitenson recognizes the challenge of putting recovery first for working parents but emphasizes the importance for those who are unstable: "We see putting recovery first as a *necessary* element in some parents struggling with frequent relapse. As individuals recover from their addictive disorders, they can often find more balance, devoting more time to their children." Evelyn, who became sober after her children were one and seven years old and had a relapse years ago, highlights that she has a "tendency to put myself at the bottom of the list and look out for their needs while neglecting my own recovery needs, which is a balancing act." She has learned from her past relapse that it is imperative to put her recovery needs first.

The identity of being a stay-at-home parent can be as strong as that of a working parent. In her memoir manuscript, *Around the Carousel*, Trish Elizabeth reflects on her own stay-at-home mother, who inspired her, remembering how dependable, punctual, and available she always was. This set an example she wanted to replicate with her children, and quitting her job when her first daughter was born was an easy decision. She writes, "By the time my second daughter was born two years later, and I was overwhelmed taking care of two small children, it never crossed my mind to look outside the home for work. I took my 'parenting job' seriously, just like my mom, and gave it everything I had." As her drinking progressed, it was hard to face that she was not fulfilling her role as she had intended, "I was not living up to my potential. I was not a good mom or a good wife . . . I loved my kids and I was grateful that I was able to devote my life to taking care of my family, but I needed more. I needed to learn how to manage my life again." In recovery, she describes how she faced her fears around shifting this view of herself and addressing her need to create a life beyond her children and home.[8]

Work/Life/Recovery Balance

When PIRs were asked how they have found work/life/recovery balance, some responses included:

- "I am not sure I'm qualified to answer this. It's something I still struggle with."
- "This has been challenging for me as it is hard to ask for help at times, which I am getting better at."
- "There is no balance with young kids."
- "I personally don't believe there is anything like balance when parenting."
- "Balance is elusive."
- "There is no such thing as balance in my opinion."
- "Still working on it!"
- "There is no balance. It's hard."

These answers represent the ongoing need ALL parents have for finding balance in their lives. PIRs have the additional challenge of internal wiring that can set them up for more extreme tendencies. While "moderation" was not possible for them with substance use, unhealthy coping can transfer to other life domains. Jackie, a social worker and mother of a young daughter and son, has found her greatest parenting challenge to be "balancing my professional identity and workload with the demands of parenthood." Valerie, a healthcare admissions specialist and mother of two young boys, explains, "As a PIR, it is the busyness of it all. I think because I went through infertility and I wanted children so much, it has been hard. I really struggled for about three years juggling work, small children, recovery, social life and asking for help. I felt guilty when I wasn't with my kids." Cathy admits, "My main strategy has always been to prioritize just my son and my work. I love my work, so this is doable for me. I don't really have a social life, and I don't care. As a writer, I spend most of my time writing and reading, and when I take a break, it's to do things for my son or to be there for him. I don't think this is workable for everyone or even a good idea necessarily. I have been especially antisocial and kind of a workaholic for the last couple of years . . . I probably still have some work to do in terms of moderation, which is related to addiction." Maggie, an executive director and mother of a young son, realized that having her son has naturally leveled out her intense focus on work and that her "hustle mentality is still there, but it has softened (or so people tell me)."

Single parents have additional pressure and responsibilities to navigate. Gina, a case manager and single mother of a son, expresses that time management has been the greatest challenge of being a working PIR, "No matter what you do, there is some element of feeling like you need to be two places at one time." Rebecca, who works at a nonprofit and has two young adult children, reports that she too struggled to find equilibrium when she was "working full-time while being a single parent."

In some cases, becoming a parent can force life domains into an organic balance. Maggie has found more stability in her career since becoming a parent, adding,

> I am no longer defined fully by my career and the hustle. I am now much more aware of the emotional availability I must have and that was something I avoided for a long time. I have had to dial back in some areas to make sure I am not coming on empty. Today, I feel emotionally balanced and still committed to my recovery and career while being a great mom. I still have priorities as it pertains to my career and honor the level of responsibility I have as a director, but I also pay attention when I need to show up as a parent.

In some cases, this controlled sense of discipline can feel constraining. David, a senior project manager with two daughters and two sons, admits, "I have become heavily reliant on routine, and at times I feel less free and spontaneous." Claire adds,

> It took a long time—years—but discovering things that brought me joy was so important. I have to find time to do those things or even do nothing at all. I have the luxury of working part-time, so I'm able to get the alone time I need. Initially, in my recovery, my sponsor and I worked a lot on not "shoulding" myself. I struggled with feeling lazy and guilty. I had to get comfortable with allowing myself the freedom of binge-watching TV. The idea of giving myself grace was more important in the beginning until I found joy in other things.

She also shares that she finds fulfillment in her work, "It's a feeling in my gut that was better than anything I got out of a bottle."

As children's needs change through the years, some parents can alter their schedules. Nancy jokingly describes, "After eight years of working part-time, and the kids getting older and less dependent on me, I began to think about what I wanted to do with the rest of my life. It felt like an early midlife crisis. There was an intense need to do something different for me as soon as I could. I ended up going back to college and getting my physical education teaching degree. After three years of full-time school, my wife jokingly wondered which would have been harder: school or an affair." Claire realized that once her son was in school, she needed to fill her time productively. She began part-time work but still needed more structure. "I looked to my community for ways to volunteer. I ended up joining a local nonprofit, which quickly led to joining another. I'm now on the board of one and have a lead role in the other. It was a slow progression, but I learned that if I take just a few steps, a lot of doors start to open."

Stay-at-home parents have unique challenges in distinguishing their personal needs from those of their family. Tracie, originally a stay-at-home mother of two daughters, now works part-time as a sales associate. She reports that her recovery has allowed her lens to shift beyond just parenting obligations. She describes, "As a stay-at-home mom, I kept busy volunteering in all school activities, PTA board positions, auction committees, helping backstage for ballet performances, etc." Tracie explains that she lacked balance between parenting and her life and that "Getting sober made me focus on myself more. I didn't do that enough when drinking and raising little kids. I thought I had to devote everything to my family. Not having a balance (outside work that fulfilled ME and had nothing to do with being a mom) turned me into a resentful and bitter person sometimes." Marilyn, initially a stay-at-home mother and now a family therapist with two grown children, recalls, "Tending to the needs of children made putting my recovery first difficult at times, but sobriety positively impacted my children. I have to say that recovery positively impacted parenthood but was not always easy to balance." Jennifer Barba believes that obtaining equilibrium for her clients is a constant challenge, with the goal being to "find a harmonious balance between personal well-being and being present for their children's needs."

Perfectionism

People struggle to slow down or to develop a work and life balance for different reasons. Perfectionism and busyness can have a compelling adrenaline buzz that allows individuals to avoid their feelings or to just sit with themselves. For PIRs with failures in their past, their sober career can increase their self-esteem and enable them to compensate. Still, others may substitute workaholism or "perfect" parenting for their past issues. Perfectionism underlies some SUDs and then surfaces in sobriety. In his book, *The Perfectionist's Handbook: Take Risks, Invite Criticism, and Make the Most of Your Mistakes*, Dr. Jeff Szymanski describes various manifestations of perfectionism that include:

- A desire for the absence of mistakes or flaws in oneself or others
- High personal standards that may be unobtainable
- An expectation of others that may be unrealistic
- A need for order and organization so that everything is in its place
- An ideal and a desire for the "just right" experience or performance
- A need to have absolutes in terms of knowledge, certainty, and safety
- To be the "best of the best" and to receive acknowledgment or accolades

One of the main takeaways from this book is that perfectionism in one life domain may be maintainable but, if applied to all areas, can become self-defeating.[9] Parenting is an area in which choosing your battles and allowing for "good enough" can improve outcomes. Jessica Valenti illustrates the often impossible ideal some parents impose: "It's this—the guilt, the self-flagellation, the pursuit of a perfection that doesn't exist—that is sucking the joy out of motherhood. It's also why the notion of parenting as 'the hardest job in the world' isn't just cold comfort we give ourselves while attending to the minutiae of mothering, but an oppressive standard making us feel worthless."[10] Joan, an insurance salesperson and mother of two girls expresses, "Parenthood has put added stress on my desire to be perfect. It hits my triggers such as frustration and being pulled in many different directions—but I can no longer have a drink once they are in bed."

Sobriety can often be a wake-up call for parents who have ignored their needs or not focused on their identity. Valenti adds, "We mock these moms as neurotic overachievers who are obsessed with their kids, but perhaps their zealous parenting is just the understandable outcome of expecting smart, driven women to find satisfaction in spit-up. All the energy that they could be—and maybe should be—spending in the public sphere is directed at their children because they have no other place to put it."[11] Tracie recognizes, "I put my perfectionist energy into parenting but wasn't fulfilled personally." Since getting sober when her daughters were ages 11 and 13, she has reexamined her need for personal achievement and has since obtained a job that she is excelling at and pursued her passion for writing. Rosemary O'Connor, PIR and author of *A Sober Mom's Guide to Recovery*, describes how her fear of failure kept her trapped, sharing, "Doing nothing meant I wouldn't fail. Then I eventually realized that doing nothing was worse than failing. The biggest risk is not risking at all. I looked around, and everyone seemed to be doing fabulous things with their lives. I was envious: he plays the guitar so well, she's a beautiful dancer, and she runs marathons. I realized it was up to me to design and live the life I really wanted."[12]

Regarding perfectionism aimed at recovery, Liz Modugno has found that "Addiction is a lifelong disease, and recovery is a lifelong change. Trying to overcompensate or be perfect in recovery quickly is unrealistic for sustained recovery. It can actually get in the way or self-sabotage it." Maggie found that she had been putting too much pressure on herself and after becoming a mother, she recognized, "I needed to be a lot gentler with myself and rely more heavily on my sponsor and support network. I have needed a lot of reminders to lower my expectations and show up where I can."

Parent Recovery Wisdom

PIRs and addiction treatment professionals highlight strategies for clarifying parenting and recovery identity as well as finding balance with work, life, and recovery. Some are listed exactly as stated by the PIRs to capture their precise message. The following suggestions are meant to provide options and are not intended to be used in their entirety.

Parenting and Recovery Identity Integration

> *"I never pictured myself with a wife and children, and there can be discomfort when seeing 'normal' people just living their lives. I fully took on the role of a parent and did the very best that I could—and love the role. I have made it more of a focus than winning over an employer and brought more into parenting and taking care of myself and being in a healthy work environment—and that is the most important thing in my life."*
>
> —Alex

- Include children in your recovery lifestyle (as deemed age appropriate).
- Openly discuss your recovery-related values.
- Make sure that your children know how important they are while making recovery and personal growth necessary parts of your life.
- Focus each day on some aspect of your recovery, no matter how seemingly insignificant.
- Gain confidence in yourself outside of your home and comfort zone (which can inspire your children).
- Stay connected to your recovery community.
- Talk with your children about what your recovery and spirituality mean to you (if appropriate).
- Socialize with another PIR so that the children can play and you can connect with another sober person or parent.
- Put any amount of time into something that brings you joy.
- Ask other parents what has worked for them.
- Talk about your feelings, even if they feel selfish.

Work/Life/Recovery Balance

> *"At the end of their life, no one ever says that they wished they had worked more and spent less time with their family. Work is important, but not at the cost of your relationships with your family members . . . especially your kids."*
>
> —Jake

- Prioritize and Plan
    - Identify a life domain you want to focus on: parenting, personal growth, career, faith/spirituality, education, or others.
    - Create SMART short-term and long-term goals (goals that are *S*pecific, *M*easurable, *A*ttainable, *R*ealistic, and *T*ime-bound).
    - Identify barriers and seek support to address them.
    - Build routine and consistency with some flexibility.
    - Create a pie chart with all life domains adding up to a total of 100 percent to visualize which areas need more or less focus (family time, work, recovery, self-care, social life, etc.).

- Realistic Expectations
    - Avoid unnecessary pressure by setting achievable goals within the constraints of parenting and other commitments.
    - Celebrate small milestones and acknowledge progress in both parenting and personal endeavors.
    - Strive for organization or take small steps toward it.
    - Let go of perfectionism when it does not benefit you.
    - Keep your focus where you have the capacity.
- Time Management
    - Efficiently manage your time by creating a schedule that includes dedicated time for parenting, self-care, work or studies, and personal goals.
    - Write down how you are using your time each day and if that matches your goals.
    - Remember that you are responsible for setting limits and boundaries around your time.
    - Recognize that there is an abundance of time to satisfy every need and desire as long as you stay vigilant and patient.
    - Determine if the problem is that you do not "have" the time or if you are not using your time efficiently.
    - Have a schedule or a shared schedule with the other parent.
- Seek Support
    - Build a reliable support system of partners, family, friends, and caregivers who can assist with childcare responsibilities, allowing you to focus on other pursuits.
    - Consider seeking guidance from a therapist, career counselor, or life coach who can offer tailored strategies and valuable insights.
    - Explore childcare services, co-parenting arrangements, and support from loved ones.
    - Ensure effective communication within the family system so that everyone's needs are met.
    - Recognize that social connection is a human need of all parents.
    - Reach out for support from other PIRs with something as simple as a text message.
    - Ask for help.
    - Allow yourself to enjoy parenting by delegating and asking for support when needed.

- Recovery and Self-Care (see chapter 5)
  - Decrease stress by practicing self-compassion and pacing.
  - Schedule "pockets" of time that could begin with just a minute and build from there.
  - Recognize that recovery involves self-care, which requires time, planning, and needs to be embedded into your life and family dynamic.
  - Figure out what amount of recovery efforts you will need to offset parenting and work.
  - Put your recovery and self first.
- Flexibility and Adaptability
  - Embrace flexibility as demands evolve.
  - Be open to revising plans and adjusting goals as needed to align with changing circumstances.
  - Allow yourself to decline activities that are not necessary.
  - Remain teachable.
  - Avoid "should-ing" yourself.

Personal Journal Entries

May 9, 2014—Eve, age 2

Eve is a blessing—so adorable, and we have a mutual understanding of the space between us where she ends and where I begin—and we work well that way.

May 4, 2016—Eve, age 4

I sometimes wonder how I will be perceived by Eve but also honor who I am and my limitations. I can only exist as a mother with other aspects to my life—outside interests, identity, stimulation. I don't feel natural in the "mother" role. I am not nurturing by nature and I am used to being taken care of in some ways while being fiercely independent in others. I admire those who are unconventional, and I often fear that I am missing out on some experience—I am not sure what. I vacillate between being content at home to restless. Patience is a struggle for me—sometimes I observe that Eve can be more caring than I can be. I don't aspire to be the "best mom" but more to create an independent child who has a happy/fulfilling/meaningful life.

Eve's younger years have been a growing experience . . . I know who I am to a point and am unwilling to make changes and sacrifices that some other mothers make.

Be here now—for tomorrow, I will change. Nothing is permanent.

5

Self-Care Is Not Optional

"I think if you never learn to self-regulate or to be kind to yourself or to endure negative feelings, all part of self-care, you may look for ways to numb out or control your feelings chemically or to just disappear from life—which is addiction."

—Cathy

WHEN HEARING THE TERM "self-care," few think of it as a life-or-death matter. It can even have a self-indulgent connotation. Self-care applies in many contexts and not solely as it relates to SUD recovery. The simplest and most literal definition is "care for oneself."[1] While this is an accurate statement, it does not encompass the wide scope of self-care required for SUD recovery. A more comprehensive definition is "The ability to care for oneself through awareness, self-control, and self-reliance in order to achieve, maintain, or promote optimal health and well-being."[2] This definition was crafted through healthcare research and considers the antecedents and consequences beyond the simplistic meaning of the words.[3] The type of self-care needed in the SUD recovery process is "The deliberate act of centering ourselves and putting our needs at the forefront of our priority list. It involves engaging in activities or practices that help reduce or manage stress, aid in our overall health and well-being, increase our energy and satisfaction, and assist in taking care of our emotional, mental, and physical health."[4]

In the context of SUD recovery, self-care is not simply about engaging in superficial healing or activities that have a temporary impact. The ideal is proper integration into a recovery lifestyle. It may include surface-level activities such as having a manicure, but it should have a broader and deeper "soul care" scope, including "taking care of ourselves in a manner that focuses on prioritizing all aspects of our health, things that help us actually survive in the world."[5]

Self-Medication

People use and abuse alcohol and substances because they want to temporarily relieve distress or change the way that they are feeling. Substances can sometimes become the only tool used when feeling celebratory, stressed, lonely, depressed, tired, and so on. Many individuals start out using substances for one reason (socializing, fun, calming) and end up using them differently over time (physical pain, mental health issues, grief). Asking someone with an SUD why they migrated toward their preferred substance often lends insight into the underlying problem. Sedating substances such as alcohol and opiates have a calming effect for those experiencing stress, anxiety, and trauma, while stimulants such as cocaine and crystal meth can provide energy and induce euphoria for those with lower moods. Drug choices are not always this simplistic, and some individuals will use *any* drug class to "get out of themselves." Over time, the substance use can turn on them and become its own source of pain while the compulsion to use continues.

Dr. Edward Khantzian and Dr. Mark Albanese researched and wrote about addiction as a form of self-medication. Their work extended this concept also to define SUD as a disorder of self-care and self-regulation. They found that those with SUDs self-medicate because they struggle to tolerate their feelings and cannot regulate their mood. Some of these deficits are so extreme that they interfere with their ability to function or even gauge that situations often associated with their substance use have become dangerous.[6] Their book *Understanding Addiction as Self-Medication* describes that "A particular drug becomes appealing when a person discovers that the short-term 'benefits' of a particular drug become necessary to overcome some facet of or problem with regulating emotions, self-esteem, and relationships. In turn, the pain and distress associated with these vulnerabilities interact with the deficits in self-care to make addiction more probable."[7]

Turning to substances as the sole source of emotion regulation and mood management demonstrates how limited those with SUDs may become in self-soothing. The concept of addiction as a disorder of self-care and self-regulation has many layers. It helps explain why many PIRs report not genuinely caring for themselves or their safety when using substances. It also touches on the underpinning of parents who use substances as their "me" time without additional strategies. This maladaptive coping mechanism is harmful each and every time it is abused.

Most PIRs responded that they did not practice self-care during their years of active addiction. Cassie, age 44 and six years sober, reflected that she engaged in more immediately gratifying behaviors and "got my nails done, went tanning, massages, and things to make myself better." David, age 47 and sober 19 years, noted that he did not actually care for himself but was constantly serving his more selfish needs. Douglas, age 42 and 14 years sober, explained that his self-focus was on external material things, including working out and having money, leading to his perception of himself as a "dressed-up trash can." Other PIRs elaborated on why they did not care for themselves:

- "I thought my self-care back then was staying high so I wouldn't have to feel depressed and anxious. Heroin was my self-care." —Cathy, age 55, sober 23 years
- "I was too numb to know what I needed." —Chris, age 40, sober 16 years
- "As an active addict, I took care of my personal hygiene but did not deal with a lot of other self-care. Managing stress, coping with boredom . . . I drank." —Joan, age 43, sober 10 years
- "When I was drinking, drinking was my self-care. . . . While I wanted to go hiking, I never had the energy to figure out a plan on how to do so. Most of my energy went into drinking." —Nancy, age 52, sober 31 years
- "I considered drinking my 'self-care.' It was the only solution I had to know how I was feeling, it was the only relief I knew. Other than that, possibly retail therapy. No healthy version of self-care. I did go to therapy, but that was primarily to seek medication." —Stacie, age 35, sober 11 years

Many expressions have made light of this substance-fueled parent time that has become socially accepted: "witching hours," "mommy juice," and "mommy's or daddy's little helper." When asked if she ever practiced self-care as a mother before getting sober, Evelyn, age 53 and 10 years sober, responded, "Not at all. Literally never. Drinking *was* my 'self-care,' my 'me time.'" Tracie, age 46 and sober over two years, added, "The occasional 'girls weekend' or dinner out with friends seemed like self-care at the time, but wasn't really because I was still drinking."

The misguided perception of substance use as caring for oneself feeds a negative cycle. Tracie says, "The pressures of parenting, not having much time to myself and not being able to set boundaries while I was drinking, made me want to drink more. As I took less and less care of myself, it didn't seem to matter if I drank at night or not." Natasha, age 36 and sober six years, recounts that her self-care "got progressively less as my addiction progressed." Lisa, age 64 and 38 years sober, explains, "During active alcoholism, 'self-care' is about feeding the addiction." Many PIRs also experienced a sense of shame and self-loathing that prevented them from having the desire and discipline to care for themselves.

These responses starkly contrast those from parents surveyed who are not in recovery. While almost all "control group" parents drink socially, they reported engaging in various forms of self-care before and after becoming parents, which included (in order of most to least frequent): exercise, hobbies, downtime, reading/writing, travel, meditation, religious practice, healing arts (massage, reiki, etc.), therapy/coaching. Only 3.6 percent reported not engaging in any form of self-care. Surprisingly, self-care reportedly declined only slightly before and after becoming parents. When asked if they used alcohol or substances to manage stress, over half responded that they did not, and about a quarter reported "sometimes." These comparisons further emphasize that those with an active SUD have a distorted sense of how best to care for themselves and manage stress.

The parents *not* in recovery were asked about the need for PIRs to engage in self-care and maintaining life balance and what they perceived the consequences could be. Many spoke about how all parents need some form of self-care, and one stated, "All human caregivers must prioritize their personal needs, to some extent, to enable them to provide care." However, a majority responded that they were concerned about the consequences for PIRs who did not care for themselves and how that could lead to relapse or losing custody of their children. They added that self-care and accessible coping skills for PIRs seem to be mandatory and something they should prioritize. Another parent not in recovery expressed, "I think the need for self-care and maintaining as much of a life balance as possible is absolutely critical for all parents, but especially parents in recovery. If his/her recovery is at risk, everything in their life, especially their ability to care for their children in the way they want and need to, is at risk."

High Stakes

Given that those with SUDs rely on substances to cope with stress, self-medicate, and even reward themselves, recovery should include learning and reprogramming new ways to manage all that was neglected. Self-care is *not* a luxury for those in recovery; it is one of the most crucial strategies to counteract previous misdirected "caring" for themselves. Evelyn warns, "I always feel like my addiction wants me last. It wants me to be wrung out, exhausted, on edge, overwhelmed, and stressed. If I'm not careful, my addiction gets really sneaky, and I take on too much or give too much of myself to people, places, and things that don't deserve or need it. I have always felt this is a way my addiction sneaks in the back door." Stacie emphasizes, "I don't know if proper self-care would have helped me not become an addict, but I know that proper self-care prevents me from feeling overwhelmed, stressed, restless, irritable, and discontented, which would most likely eventually lead me to a drink or a drug."

Early sobriety involves redirecting the energy put forth into self-destructive behaviors toward wellness. It is a slow and often uncomfortable process—yet imperative. It is a time for individuals to learn how to listen to their needs and implement the most appropriate coping strategies—a trial and error process. It can be even further complicated when someone is a parent and has their children's needs to attend to. Chris admits that when he got sober, "I had all the time in the world to work on myself. I doubt I would have gotten sober later with kids." However, PIRs who got sober after having children were forced to figure out creative ways to care for their children and meet their own needs.

Parents not in recovery have a lower sense of urgency but a healthy sense of priority regarding self-care. Survey results indicate that they have engaged in various self-care pursuits before and after becoming parents. Just over half reported that they consider self-care and wellness a priority, and less than one-third responded that it was "sometimes" a priority. However, when asked to rate the potential impact of not prioritizing or maintaining self-care and wellness on a scale from 1 (no impact) to 10 (life-threatening), over 50 percent responded with 5 or 7, 13.6 percent with 8 and 9 percent with 9. When asked what the consequences (they could respond with multiple answers) would be for their mental and physical health if they did not engage in self-care, almost 90 percent answered that they would experience stress, 60 percent decreased overall patience, 50 percent decreased parenting patience and ability, 35 percent anger, and 25 percent mental health symptoms; most notable, only 10 percent reported that they would increase their alcohol or substance usage. When not taking care of themselves mentally, physically, or spiritually or when not managing stress effectively, two-thirds indicated that their children would "sometimes" or "not" notice or sense this shift.

In contrast, if the responses of PIRs were the same as parents not in recovery, PIRs would be at higher risk of relapse and dysregulation of their emotional sobriety. They have so much to lose. Many PIRs feel an increased sense of commitment to their recovery after becoming a parent because the stakes have become higher and could impact so many. In contrast, parents not in recovery may have less patience or more anger—but the short-term consequences would not necessarily be devastating or life-threatening.

Self-Care Phases

How PIRs care for themselves varies based on recovery stages. The five recovery stages (described in chapter 1) are stabilization, deepening, connectedness, integration, and fulfillment. The characteristics of these stages correlate with self-care practices for many PIRs. Typical practices for PIRs in the "stabilization" and "deepening" stages included spending a lot of time at self-help meetings with sober peers and remaining vigilant about their recovery efforts. "Self-care in early sobriety was mostly spending time with other recovering people. I just felt so much relief being around others who understood and who were walking or had walked this path before me. Eventually, I started exercising, eating better, and sleeping better, which really helped stress," Evelyn recalls. Tracie emphasizes, "I went to meetings every day for over four months and my family knew that at 10 am, it was MY hour, and after that, we would do something else. I hiked a lot with my dog and spent a lot of time out in nature. I took naps when I could. I cried when I needed to. I spent time with other sober women."

Some PIRs in early recovery have difficulty being alone and managing downtime. It can take several years for them to "downshift" their mind and body to adjust to a sober rhythm. Joan remembers that she "ate healthy, worked out, kept myself VERY busy, no alone time, and put myself first in deciding what I did." She found her voice and could finally express her needs to loved ones. Jackie, age 38 and 14 years sober, admits, "I would sometimes get my nails or hair done, but overall, I would say my concept of self-care was not great. I was addicted to the stress response and always taking a lot on my plate; free time never felt comfortable or 'safe' for me. As I have gotten older, I choose to spend a lot more time in solitude, nurturing my relationship with self and a higher power, as well as listening to what my body needs." Maggie, age 35 and sober for 15 years, also struggled with being by herself in early sobriety, adding, "In the beginning of my recovery, my self-care consisted of connection to other people. I was not in a position to spend a lot of time alone with my own thoughts, so I engaged in a lot of recovery-based activities. Everything from meetings to service commitments and larger events with friends. I always prioritized good sleep hygiene because that was something imperative to my recovery."

The earlier stages, including the "connectedness" stage of years three to five, are the foundation for longer-term recovery and growth. Natasha explains that the rigid self-care and recovery schedule she engaged in early on taught her the importance of taking care of herself. "If I do not do that, I have nothing to give to others. I am pouring from an empty cup. So, I really try to prioritize taking care of myself first, which leads to having much more to give to my family." Violet, age 38 and sober 18 years, expresses that becoming a parent has elevated her recovery from sticking solely to self-help meetings and socializing to "therapy, meditation, spiritual practice, eating healthy, maintaining healthy relationships, and working out consistently." Alex, age 43 and sober for 12 years, also agrees that becoming a parent led him to get more creative with his recovery schedule and to consider his family with more deliberate planning.

As PIRs move into the "integration" and "fulfillment" stages of longer-term recovery, their self-care typically evolves and broadens. Sharon, age 55 and sober 24 years describes, "In early sobriety, self-care simply meant 'sticking to the script' and doing what was in front of me. Going to work and getting to a meeting. Period. This changed around year 10 when I began to trust myself a bit more and sobriety allowed me to broaden my foundation." Maggie affirms, "As I became more comfortable in my own recovery, I started to expand my self-care to meditative practices, alone time, exercise, and time in nature." Gina, age 41 and sober 7 years emphasizes, "I used to think that self-care was just external, and now it has transformed into allowing myself to say no. Especially with the parenting stuff. 'No' is a complete sentence."

Having a child(ren) adds layers to life that consume additional energy and resources. With that in mind, an individual's self-care and recovery plan before parenting will inevitably shift. Jackie explains, "Becoming a parent has highlighted the necessity for me to slow down and prioritize my own nervous system regulation as a form of self-care. Creating space for me to have alone time where I can exercise, meditate, or journal." Through experimentation, Natasha discovered that "Hiking, and other outdoor adventures in all four seasons, has literally saved my sanity as a parent. I remember when I realized that being active outside in nature literally allows parenting anxiety to lift off my body. Getting those endorphins from exercise changes my brain and allows me to see situations much more clearly." For others, the sense of urgency of early recovery can motivate more significant self-care efforts that wane as parenthood progresses. Evelyn expresses, "It's much easier for me to put self-care in the back seat now than it was when I was in early recovery. Usually, when I'm feeling really stressed or burned out, it's not because there is so much more going on (although sometimes that's why); it's because I have taken my eye off self-care."

Barriers

Many parents talk about how they have no time for themselves or that they don't have the drive to focus on their own needs after caring for their family. Other parents may not have the same struggle with this balance. This applies to parents both in and out of recovery. Several factors must be considered to fully understand what prevents parents from caring for themselves. In her book *All Joy and No Fun*, Jennifer Senior discusses the social pressure on parents to overcommit and overschedule with the illusion that this will afford their children the best life opportunities. This parenting culture revolves around and puts all children first, without much consideration for the impact on parents, "As far as children are concerned, there is no such thing as excess. If improving their children's lives means running themselves ragged—and *thinking* themselves ragged—then so be it. Parents will do it. Their children will deserve nothing less."[8] Jackie elaborates, "I know there is a philosophy around parenting in which your children come before anything, but I have to fill my own cup first—not in a selfish way, but in order to pour into my children and spouse." Another source of overscheduling and over-functioning for PIRs can be fueled by guilt. Jill Griffin, LCSW, also notes that some of her clients do not feel worthy of taking care of themselves because of their past addiction. They try to compensate for lost time by overextending themselves and resisting slowing down. She suggests that to know how to "do" self-care, clients must foster a relationship with their bodies and minds to recognize when they feel out of balance.

Parents, and especially mothers, are often expected to have an endless well to draw upon for their family. This can create a time conflict for a parent who gets sober or is already a PIR. Challenging thought and behavior patterns are often needed to manage family responsibilities. Violet describes a radical shift in her belief system: "I do consider my kids' needs first at times, and that leaves me feeling empty and depleted. This is now one of the non-negotiables in my life. The foundation of my self-care is rooted in mind, body, and spirit on a daily basis. I have found I am at my highest self if these are maintained. . . . It took some time to realize that the mommy guilt comes from a lack of connection with my kids. Not the 'doing' for them, but the connection." The quality of the time spent with children seems to be as important as the amount.

Molly Ashcroft, CADC, ICADC, feels that some of the responsibility for supporting self-care for PIRs also lies with mental health professionals "to support, encourage, and identify realistic ways to promote self-care and share the imperative nature of it to create a long-term recovery plan. Our society teaches a 'grind-like' mentality and rarely offers room to discuss what creates burnout, stress, relapse, and mental health problems at large." Mental health and addiction treatment professionals should assume that clients may be overscheduled, overworked, and overstimulated—and that the slowing down process can take time and work against societal norms. Many PIRs need to learn that it is possible to work and live efficiently while embracing self-care to maintain stable recovery. Cassie expresses a different perspective, "I can honestly see it more in my recovery than when I was actively drinking. When I was drinking, all I thought about was myself, and I made sure I made time to take care of myself. In my recovery, I have difficulty finding the balance, especially since becoming a parent. I am either working or parenting." When she was actively using substances, Cassie was more self-absorbed, and her life was smaller. Since getting sober, she has been operating at a higher level in her career and as a mother, leaving her less time to connect with herself.

Active addiction involves many selfish behaviors and can hurt loved ones. Those in recovery, especially early recovery, need to take time for healing, which consists of focusing again on themselves. This can put a strain on loved ones and family systems. The recovery process can feel like a full-time job, which can be overwhelming, especially for those who have become sober during parenthood. The number of hours in the day is finite, and PIRs must get creative with their schedules. Valerie, age 42 and sober for 24 years, adds that she struggled with "the guilt around addiction takes us away from family, then sobriety does the same thing." David has felt guilt around "self-time" and finding a balance that has fewer triggers for trauma and anxiety. "The guilt is that I don't want to look back and wish I spent more time with the boys and less on myself." In contrast, Alex expresses, "You are the best if you put yourself first—then you are the best parent, spouse, employee." Molly Ashcroft has observed that significant barriers can include family systems that guilt and shame PIRs about the time they take for themselves. She also notes that childcare issues can contribute and are sometimes related to resentment within the family around the time needed for recovery and self-care. Jill Griffin often processes how self-care was modeled in the PIRs' family of origin and how that may impact their concept or guilt around taking time for themselves in recovery. This information can be helpful in terms of challenging old belief systems and creating strategies for restructuring what balance and wellness mean to them now.

The American parenting landscape has many different racial, cultural, and socioeconomic statuses. Parental roles passed along from generation to generation also have a powerful impact and should not be minimized. Additionally, varying perspectives around self-care and gender norms can impact the ease at which PIRs can make changes. Some view mothers as the backbone of the family and believe they should shoulder all burdens while simultaneously caring for themselves. Other expectations placed on mothers are that they should repress their own feelings and sacrifice their needs for the sake of the family system.[9] In contrast, men in many cultures and family systems are expected to be stoic, neither vulnerable nor needing emotional support. "Self-care" can be viewed as selfish or unnecessary, but this can be a misinterpretation, particularly when applied to PIRs. These factors should be considered, along with cultural sensitivity, during the recovery process.

Parent Recovery Wisdom

The following strategies are from PIRs themselves and addiction treatment professionals. These approaches highlight self-care and soul-care strategies in various life domains. Some are listed exactly as stated by the PIRs to capture their tone and message. The following suggestions are meant to provide options and are not intended to be used in their entirety.

Physical/Behavioral

- EXERCISE! (a unanimous suggestion)
- Move a muscle, change a thought.
- Strive to get the hours of sleep you need to be at your best.
- Eat a healthy, nutritious diet.
- Create a behavioral schedule and structure for your days and weeks.
- Perform self-soothing activities.
- Be careful not to overschedule.
- Say "no" to events that are optional.
- Regularly schedule childcare or arrange other options that allow time for personal needs. Examples include childcare swaps or support from family members.

- Go to the movies or other favorite activities alone.
- "Schedule" personal time into your calendar and/or family calendar in advance.
- Find exercise options that you can do with your child (e.g., stroller running, hiking, going to the beach or park, practicing yoga).
- Explore the healing arts (massage, reiki, energy healing, yoga, etc.).
- Drink tea or other comforting and calming hot beverages.
- Walk daily solo or with a friend in a new or familiar place.

Psychological and Emotional

- Engage in therapy with an addiction specialist who can address underlying mental health issues.
- Take the time to find the right "fit" therapist; remain patient and persistent in that process.
- Evolve continually with micro-changes that you can maintain.
- Engage in conversations about recovery and wellness.
- Be sure family members are supported (therapy, self-help, coaching).
- Exercise for both physical and mental health.
- Spend time with animals.
- Read or listen to self-help and inspirational books/audiobooks.
- Engage in meaningful hobbies.
- Journal, using either a structured template or a stream of consciousness technique.
- Find your joy!

Recovery-Related Socializing

- Recovery is about connection with others; addiction is about disconnection.
- Join a healthy social group (sports club, hiking, skiing, book club, etc.).
- End your isolation in any healthy way possible.
- Join parent groups that you may connect with.
- Attend wellness retreats.
- Find balance with healthy socializing and honing your ability to be alone or in a quiet environment.
- Be present during time with your family.
- Be HONEST when people ask how you are doing.

- Expect that others may not understand the need to make so many social changes.
- Seek out people who respect your recovery and around whom you can be yourself.
- Attend in-person and virtual self-help meetings (see resources section at the end of the book).
- Assure you feel emotionally safe in your social circle.
- Create a group chat with other PIRs to open up lines of communication.
- Find your recovery "tribe."
- Get involved in a community of people who ascribe to a substance-free lifestyle (for reasons of health, religion, or related to recovery).
- Push yourself to be social and connected to the outside world, especially when children are young.
- Cultivate closeness with a few people in your life whom you can confide in and trust.
- Spend time with friends doing FUN things.
- Share true feelings at self-help meetings.
- Go somewhere with your child, even if it feels overwhelming to think about.
- Meet with friends outside self-help meetings.

Internal and External Environments

- Figure out where you find peace internally or externally.
- Set boundaries about who can enter your home.
- Create a substance-free home (especially in early recovery).
- Try to keep your home organized.
- Be honest with yourself and others about your comfort level with alcohol or other substances in the house.
- Carve out a quiet space in your home where you can retreat when needed.
- Take a trip, locally or far away.
- Drive different routes to avoid "ghosts of the past" (e.g., liquor stores or pot shops).
- Spend some time outside every day.
- Clean your home of any wine, beer, or shot glasses and any paraphernalia or other reminders of past use.

- Stay away from environments that center around drinking and substance use.

Spiritual/Religious

- Try different spiritual practices.
- Determine how best to channel your spiritual nature.
- Set up a sacred space in your home with meaningful objects and literature.
- Seek knowledge about spirituality and religion.
- Engage in and learn about breathwork for stress management and emotional grounding.
- Engage in some form of personal growth that honors you.
- Remain open-minded, curious, and teachable.
- Accept that you may not know "what" you believe in.
- Find humility.
- Begin meditating with one minute of silence or a guided meditation and then work toward being comfortable with increasing the amount of time.
- Immerse yourself in nature (urban and rural) and connect with something greater than yourself.
- Choose your own value system of spirituality that fits with you.
- Find spirituality through other people or their beliefs.
- Discover something to believe in outside of yourself.
- Practice yoga in person or virtually and/or simply take time to stretch and relieve muscle tension.
- Pray.
- Write gratitude lists.
- Explore religious institutions.
- Include your child in spiritual practices.
- Read a small paragraph, an excerpt, or a daily reflection to start the day.

Personal Journal Entries

Below are just a sampling of my journal entries expressing my joys and challenges as a mother. I often felt that other parents were having an easier time of it and have since learned that is not the norm. During these times, I began to understand why the "mommy-drinking culture" was gaining steam and how alluring that quick fix could appear. As a PIR, that was not an option for me, and I was working hard—really hard—to explore healthy ways to navigate my own nature, parenting role, and recovery growth. I made a point to travel alone to a wellness and spiritual retreat and to take that quiet time to reflect on what I needed to change and focus on for my emotional sobriety. This time away was intentionally hard—not using my phone, being completely alone, sitting silently during meals, meditating, and practicing deep breathing and yoga. The silence could be painful. But leaving the everyday chaos and noise to sit with myself for several days always left me feeling clear-headed, refreshed, and focused on what I needed to do once I returned home.

September 7, 2013—Eve, 20 months old

I had a really hard day today with Eve. She is becoming more willful but has also been "fussy," and I am not the most patient person. . . . Funniest are her words/phrases, "DO IT!" means "I want to do it myself!"

I honestly have times when I wasn't able to escape or be by myself, and I can see how mothers who drink can get into bad patterns. The constancy of parenthood is difficult for me at times.

September 10, 2013

It is hard to have patience for me at times. I still feel the need to have my own time or downtime, and that doesn't always happen when I need it.

January 11, 2014—Eve, two years old

Recovery focus:

- Be less reactive.
- Increase mindfulness with Eve.
- Increase and maintain spiritual practice (meditation, spiritual classes).

- Do not take emotions out on others.
- Do more regular self-inventory.

October 7, 2017

Being at Kripalu (spiritual retreat center) each time reminds me of the first time I came here. Both the peace I felt and also the anxiety I experienced from being away from home by myself. I am now at peace here in all ways.

I realize changes will always need to be made, and the quiet here allows me to organize myself enough to acknowledge and find willingness. Changes I have committed to make are:

1. Go to bed earlier, meditate and read before bed.
2. Stretch and do breathwork twice daily.
3. Implement mindful Mom and Eve time.
4. Make some Ayurveda dietary changes.
5. Continue to explore volunteer options that are in nature or with the Red Cross.
6. Attend a weekly meditation group.
7. No phone use after 8 p.m.

6

Coping with Hard Times

"This too shall pass."

—Proverb

HARD TIMES THROUGHOUT LIFE are unavoidable. Yet human nature leads people to have an aversion to psychological and physical discomfort. Many tend to look for shortcuts to either cope or return to homeostasis. Situations also impact individuals in unique ways. At some point, everyone will encounter a roadblock that will push them to seek a solution. Solutions range from "living with" the discomfort to applying healthy coping mechanisms to numbing out the pain with addictive behaviors. Because PIRs cannot engage in substance use as an option, they must find alternative strategies.

Stress and Microstressors

PIRs described the most stressful situations that they have experienced during parenthood:

- "Working outside the home with two small children. I breastfed and pumped for their first years. I was getting up at night, and it was exhausting." —Valerie, age 42, with two young sons

- "Limited income in early recovery caused me to worry about covering the rent each month or having enough food." —Sharon, age 55, with a grown son and daughter
- "I had a debilitating groin injury that lasted a span of four years. It made day-to-day living very uncomfortable and, at times, painful. I had gastritis for almost two years. Both of these ailments had me questioning my will to live." —Mason, age 43, with a teenage son and two younger children
- "When my oldest was 12, he needed his tonsils out. During testing, they thought his blood was showing signs of leukemia. After several rounds of tests and waiting, it was determined it must have just been a virus." —Laura, age 64, with two grown children
- "When my daughter was born, I had two babies under three and a full-time, emotionally demanding job. My life became nearly untenable, and my self-care went out the window." —Claire, age 40, with two young sons
- "I was fired from the company I started with almost no parachute." —Chris, age 40, with two young daughters
- "I had a major surgery when my children were six and three. I was unable to walk on my own for two months and had a long recovery after that. The feeling of not being independent to care for myself or my family the way I was used to was extremely stressful." —Jackie, age 38, with a young daughter and son

While the impact of these events varies from person to person, the experience of stress is universal. Most individuals know what "stress" means to them or their baseline level and responses. Stress can be defined as "a physical, chemical, or emotional factor that causes bodily or mental tension and may be a factor in disease causation."[1] It can be categorized as mild, moderate, or severe and varies in the time frame, source, and impact. It can also trigger the fight or flight response of the sympathetic nervous system, which can lead to an increase in heart rate, metabolism, blood pressure, temperature, and more.

The general perception of stressors is that they are large and prominent. In contrast, microstressors are more subtle and insidious. They are small, manageable, and appear to be usual "bumps in the road." Many individuals are accustomed to them, taught to deal with or ignore them and do not register their impact. However, microstressors accumulate, with the result creating domino effects. Large stressors are more obvious and elicit more sympathy and understanding from others. In contrast, microstressors may even seem positive or justifiable. These stressors can slide by the nervous system undetected, not even registering as harmful.[2] They are also rampant in the parenting world. An example is a PIR who checked their email at 9:00 p.m. and stayed up late working on a last-minute (but not emergent) request from their boss (microstress). They woke up late the next morning and started the day off already feeling behind. They skipped their morning workout to get the children to school on time (immediate ripple effect). They were late to the office and still preoccupied with the topic of their boss's email, because they did not have time to clear their mind with their usual exercise regimen (secondary ripple). They came home from work tired and irritable, with little to offer their family emotionally (tertiary ripple). The simple act of checking work emails in the evening set off a domino of microstress effects that continued into the next day and evening.

Our minds and bodies are accustomed to looking for recognizable stressors. Our body wants to maintain internal homeostasis and uses the fight or flight mechanism to acclimate when needed. Microstressors are like stealth aircrafts that evade detection by the brain's internal radar. However, although the brain isn't managing or limiting these stresses, the body still registers responses. This can lead to even more severe consequences because there isn't a "body budget" set aside for these microstressors as there is for more obvious large stressors. The cumulative impact can blindside individuals.[3] While it is essential to manage significant life stressors, there is also value in addressing the more subtle microstressors.

Research has been ongoing on the negative impact of stress on mental health, physical wellness, and substance use. Dr. Herbert Benson, a pioneer in the field of mind/body medicine, conducted research as well as treated patients with stress-related illnesses. *The Wellness Book: The Comprehensive Guide to Maintaining Health and Treatment Stress-Related Illnesses* and his subsequent work describe how stress impacts chronic health conditions, infertility, and cancer recovery. The treatment groups provided related "relaxation response" mind and body strategies to decrease client stress levels and increase their healing.[4] Other research connects past and present stressors with an increase in substance usage. The National Institutes of Health found that personality, heredity, and lifestyle contribute to how an individual handles stress. People are resilient when they can respond quickly to pressure and rebound quickly from the activation of their sympathetic nervous system. But the personality characteristics of resilience are in stark contrast with those associated with an increased risk of SUD. Individuals with a history of alcohol use disorder, in particular, may have more difficulty dealing with stress factors that can lead to alcohol use problems.[5] Additionally, the impact of long-term heavy alcohol and substance use can alter brain chemistry. These findings add to the need for PIRs, especially in early sobriety, to be vigilant in learning healthy coping skills to strengthen their resiliency muscles. In contrast, the survey conducted for parents not in recovery asked if they used alcohol and substances to relieve stress and 53.6 percent reported "no," 35.7 percent reported "sometimes," and 10.7 percent reported "yes." This demonstrates that parents who are not dependent on substances to manage stress may have developed a greater resiliency or a coping process that allowed them to reach homeostasis through other methods.

Parenting is an example of a situation that can be favorable but at the same time create enormous stressors and microstressors. PIRs may be grateful for being a parent but still struggle with the everyday realities. Sometimes it is too much of a good thing—too many activities, commitments, and obligations—and not enough time. "We often don't stop to realize our Supermom role's impact on our children. Not only do they grow up believing that moms must do it all, but most kids these days are over-scheduled themselves, pulled from one place to another. . . . It's no wonder our kids are stressed out, exhausted, and cranky—just like their mothers—or that they, too, turn to alcohol and drugs."[6] Single parents have the same level of responsibility but often do not have a partner to offer financial or other support. Those who co-parent have the additional layer of coordinating with the other parent.[7]

Difficult Life Circumstances

When individuals become sober from an SUD, they are left to deal with "life on life's terms." Individuals in early sobriety can believe they are exempt from hard times because they have positively changed their lives. While some experience a "pink cloud" or euphoric feeling following their newfound sobriety, this cloud may evaporate with the reality of the wreckage of their past or current life hardships. Liz Modugno, LCSW, LADC, prepares clients for challenges by encouraging them to "Think about a professional sports team and their intense practice regimen or a soldier that conditions their body and mind before battle. Both the athlete and the soldier work daily to learn skills, lean on their teammates and peers, and prepare themselves for their individual battles. Sobriety is similar. You are working day in and day out to create a foundation of support and skills to overcome difficult and stressful times."

PIRs with stable sobriety implement adaptive skills to replace the maladaptive one of substance use. PIRs share how they were initially overwhelmed by the following life stressors but were able to *apply* strategies they learned in real time to adapt and heal.

Challenges with Children

Parents are courageous. They bring vulnerable children into the world, knowing they may face difficulties that could break their hearts or bring up their own past trauma. There can be comfort for PIRs in knowing they are not alone in their experience or in hearing how others have managed these situations.

Parents often feel that their children's issues reflect the quality of their parenting or themselves personally. However, each child has their own nature, even when parents have multiple children. Claire, sober for six years, found out her son had a learning disability in kindergarten. She was surprised by her own reaction, in that "I felt like it was a reflection of my ability as an occupational therapist or lack thereof—like I had to fix it right away and that I was an imposter and doing everything wrong." This led her to attempt to control everything around her, including the school. Through her recovery work, she recognized that her "character defects and lack of spiritual fortitude led me to alcoholism in the first place." She began to apply recovery and spiritual principles, and her entire approach and experience shifted.

Similarly, Nancy, sober for 31 years, spoke candidly about her hardships with a daughter who smoked marijuana regularly when she entered high school. Nancy explains, "I felt like I didn't know her anymore. Smoking was in direct opposition to our family values. I went to a family therapist who works with children using substances. She was so great! I worked hard at not reacting to things my daughter said and did, and I would call my wife or a friend to talk about things. One of the most important things I did was take care of myself—we started going to Al-Anon meetings (separately), and I started hiking around this difficult parenting time. Getting outside in the woods year-round became my medicine. All these activities helped the parenting anxiety lift right out of me—I would see it lift off my arms as I hiked up a mountain. It was an incredible release." Nancy's recovery allowed her to proactively seek therapeutic, self-help and self-care support.

Health

Health and wellness are essential aspects of recovery. Newly sober individuals sometimes have past health issues they are unaware of or have previously avoided addressing. Others were concerned about their health yet ignored the negative impact that their SUD may have had. Some individuals with longer-term recovery have found effective ways to manage acute or chronic health issues.

Jackie, sober for 14 years, had a major surgery that led to two years of discomfort and co-occurring health problems. It was a daily practice to prevent herself from falling into a place of self-pity and fear. However, she was able to reach for the tools she had learned. She explains, "My recovery has helped me foster a spiritual connection that is unshakeable and available to me through difficult times. I also have a large support network available to me through whatever difficulty I may face. The value of having people in recovery who surround me is that I can usually find someone who has had the experience before me and can walk me through it."

Valerie, sober for 24 years, reports that the most challenging time in her recovery was the three-year period when she was dealing with infertility. She reflects that it almost led her to relapse, as the mental obsession to drink suddenly returned. She was angry and resentful at her higher power and acknowledged, "I felt like I was doing everything right, so why am I not getting the results?" After extreme suffering, she recognized that she needed to develop a more mature relationship with a higher power that was not based on bargaining. Following this spiritual shift, she has been blessed with two boys.

Loss

Many PIRs have experienced the loss of loved ones who had SUDs, as they were part of their family or social circle. This can lead some to wonder how they have been spared while others who had used substances have passed away—survivors' guilt. Human loss can be traumatic and lead to a lengthy grief process. While PIRs may have escaped those emotions in the past, sobriety forces them to deal with them directly.

Cassie, sober for 15 years, experienced the sudden loss of both her mother and mother-in-law. She expresses, "They provided an enormous support network for us, and we suddenly lost that. I was more easily able to do things for myself and my recovery with the support of a parent that I trusted to care for my child while I cared for myself." She has been unable to replace the emotional support or care and continues feeling this void in their lives. However, her sobriety allowed her to step up after her mother's passing to help her father make important decisions while protecting her recovery.

Sam has been sober for 45 years and, surprisingly, he became sober on the same day as his wife. After 30 years of marriage, his wife was diagnosed with an inoperable brain aneurysm that led to the loss of her long-term memory and eventually to her passing. While Sam had been slowly mourning the loss of his wife because of her personality changes, he had also been her primary caregiver for several years. After her death, he received tremendous support from his adult children and support network. He took time for his wellness, hobbies, immersed himself in learning new aspects of his religion and continued involvement in his self-help program. He also took up new sports, such as biking and surfing, and was dedicated to ongoing growth to help his grieving process.

Divorce, Separation, and Relationship Issues

Ideally, homes are safe spaces, and partners are intended to provide emotional security. However, the opposite experience can be created by divorce, separation, and relationship issues. The comfort a partner may have provided in the past is suddenly replaced with an adversarial dynamic that impacts the entire family system. Some PIRs become sober and realize that they can no longer stay in a partnership, substance use may have had an irreversible negative impact or the relationship has run its course.

Cathy, sober for 23 years, identifies her divorce and subsequent five-year custody battle as the most challenging and traumatic time in her recovery. She summarized, "My ex-husband's new wife was abusive to my child, and while I had about 95 percent custody, the little time my son spent with them was damaging and terrifying. I was in this fight for my son's well-being, constantly strategizing and figuring out how to keep him safe." She felt confident in her sobriety and resiliency even during the darkest times. Cathy highlights, "I know that having survived seven years of heroin addiction and being clean for 23 years means I can get through anything."

Trish Elizabeth, in her manuscript *Around the Carousel*, captured the sense of fear and disorientation when facing a divorce in early sobriety, writing, "Yet moments after one of those phone calls (to lawyers), I could be hiding in my room, curled in a ball, tears flowing, wondering how I was going to survive. And sober—damn—I really had to stay sober now. No way I would let alcohol get in the way of my negotiations with him regarding our daughters."[8] She described the security she felt in playing the victim and blaming those around her for why she drank and for her marriage problems. However, Trish's recovery and self-help group gave her the confidence, skills, and support to focus on herself and work through this situation in a healthy manner. She described a profound shift in perspective around her view of her marriage. She stated, "It was completely self-centered of me to believe that I was the only one who caused problems in the marriage, leaving it up to me to solve them. It was never all his fault, and it was never all mine. I began to see that marriage is complicated and never as simple as a one-sided issue."[9]

The Pandemic

The COVID-19 pandemic was an unprecedented period from when the World Health Organization declared the novel coronavirus outbreak to be a global pandemic on March 11, 2020,[10] until the federal public health emergency ended on May 11, 2023.[11] The endless number of stressors put an enormous strain on many parents and their children vocationally, educationally, emotionally, financially, and physically.

Some of these specific stressors included: social isolation, school closures, temporary and permanent business closures, lack of in-person religious and spiritual services, fears of illness and death, changing and contradictory government mandates, vaccine confusion, masking requirements, job loss, travel restrictions, and overall change fatigue.

Key research findings included:

- 40 percent of U.S. adults in 2020 reported struggling with mental health or substance use, and 13 percent started or increased substance use to cope with stress.[12]
- Parents with children younger than 18 were more stressed and anxious than those who were child-free.[13]
- In 2020, on an incremental scale of 1 to 10, the average stress level for parents was 6.7 (almost half reported scores between 8 to 10), while child-free individuals reported an average stress level of 5.5.[14]
- 49.3 percent of mothers of children under 18 reported symptoms of anxiety and depression compared with 40.3 percent of men.[15]
- Women increased their heavy drinking days by 41 percent compared to before the pandemic.[16]
- 25 percent of essential workers started or increased substance use to cope with stress or emotions related to the pandemic compared with 11 percent of nonessential workers.[17]
- The rates of depression *tripled* from 6.2 million to 17.3 million, with a more significant impact on those with lower economic means.[18]

While the government and media focused with tunnel vision on the tragic medical component, the mental health and substance use impacts and downstream effects were largely ignored. What followed has been a behavioral health epidemic that has remained elevated for years after the pandemic began. A Kaiser Family Foundation survey found that 90 percent of U.S. adults believed the country faced an ongoing mental health crisis—spawned by isolation and loneliness, job loss, financial insecurity, financial instability, illness, and grief.[19] Sadly, the rates of adults reporting anxiety and depressive disorder symptoms did not subside at the end of the pandemic, showing 35.9 percent in April 2020, 39.3 percent in February 2021, 31.5 percent in February 2022 and 32.2 percent in February 2023. The highest rates of 52.8 percent were among individuals who had experienced household job loss and 49.9 percent among 18 to 24-year-olds.[20] Even more stunning is comparing these statistics to a 2019 benchmark which found that only 8.1 percent of adults 18 and older had reported symptoms of anxiety disorder, 6.5 percent reported symptoms of depressive disorder, and 10.8 percent reported symptoms of anxiety disorder or depressive disorder.[21]

In her book, *Screaming on the Inside: The Unsustainability of American Motherhood*, Jessica Grose emphasizes the amount of stress that parents were under during the pandemic, writing, "A lot of moms I have interviewed have found that this lack of personal time means that their pre-pandemic coping mechanisms are not available to them, which makes them feel more stressed and less able to deal with the pressures of work and care stacked on top of each other."[22] Jill Griffin, LCSW, LADC, observed in her practice, "The extreme pressure of the pandemic has exacerbated people's anxiety, fear, and depression. Parents were expected to work while also helping their children with schoolwork. The demands were not realistic for most, on top of many typical outlets for self-care being taken away. Many people in recovery lost their in-person meetings and fellowship. I heard many people relapsing during the pandemic and dying from overdoses." Nancy Nitenson, MD, shared that for clients in active addiction,

> The pandemic was catastrophic in so many ways, and it's clear that substance use skyrocketed. In screening patients for my practice, the calls usually started with, "Well, it all started during the pandemic . . ." The truth is there was usually a problem well before the pandemic started, but the imposed lockdown resulted in problem drinking that loved ones could no longer ignore as they witnessed the free-fall as families spent more time together. Some families were drinking together at times, in sort of a shared denial, having happy hour each night.

Molly Ashcroft, CADC, ICADC, works in an inpatient SUD treatment setting and saw that "The difficulties among parents increased tremendously. A few challenges included: increased substance and alcohol abuse due to financial fears, health concerns, lack of connection, grief and loss, lack of family contact." She also noted that parents had barriers to accessing inpatient and residential care due to limited childcare resources specific to the pandemic. Dan Lynch, LADC-1, CIP founder and president of Lynch Wellness Professional Group, licensed alcohol and drug counselor and interventionist, found that "PIRs faced a high risk for regression, particularly parents who were not confident in their parenting roles were really tested during this time as they had little or no support with childcare."

Multitasking was taken to new levels for many parents. Violet, a working mother with three children, shared, "I felt the overwhelm of having children and trying to shift gears from being a business owner on the go to working remotely and learning how to teach my kids online school." Mason, an EMT with three school-age children, noted, "My children were at home all day every day and struggling with online school. It was an incredibly challenging time to navigate." Alex, a working father who stayed home with his children, said, "It was the toughest time of my entire sobriety. I was at home with the kids for the first two months, and I was a parent, a teacher, and an employee." Some PIRs or their children could not focus or felt more social anxiety symptoms with video conferencing. This lessened the effectiveness of academic, work, and self-help virtual meeting attendance. Stacie, a working mother of three school-age children, found the virtual self-help meetings very hard because she has attention deficit hyperactivity disorder (ADHD). She explains that she needed in-person meetings, and "Thankfully, I found a group of women doing outdoor socially distanced in-person meetings. I think that helped me a ton."

Many parents had to reach out for support in finding childcare options to function effectively. Jackie, a social worker and mother of two school-age children, explains, "I worked in the hospital during the pandemic, and my husband worked from home with the children. It was a stressful time for the family until we were blessed to find childcare that took the pressure off both of us. Both of my kids remained in person in school during the pandemic, and thankfully we did not see long-term effects such as social anxiety or learning challenges." Joan, a working mother with two school-age daughters, says that she "reached out to my family system. We went to my parents during the week along with my sister and her children. They helped with online school and kept me involved in exercising. I always make sure I'm not alone."

Dr. Nitenson found that the in-person human connection continued to be crucial for individuals struggling with relapse during the pandemic, emphasizing, "I suggested outdoor self-help meetings for patients that were at high risk and even in-person meetings on occasion for patients that were chronically relapsing. It's all about risk assessment. People die from drug overdoses, not just COVID-19. And while parents found online meetings helpful, it affected the rate at which meaningful friendships were made with others in recovery."

The COVID-19 pandemic also led to some positive changes and realizations for PIRs. Jennifer Barba, LCSW, describes, "Despite these challenges—resilience and adaptation have played crucial roles in overcoming them. PIRs who sought alternative support systems, embraced virtual platforms for therapy and meetings, and engaged in self-care practices have shown remarkable strength and perseverance. Additionally, the support of family members, online recovery communities, and innovative approaches to treatment have been invaluable in helping individuals navigate these difficult times and maintain their recovery goals." Molly Ashcroft observed that more people realized they needed inpatient SUD treatment and,

> We saw an increased number of PIRs access care that may have never reached out for help if it weren't for the pandemic. Many PIRs entered treatment for the first time due to having much more accountability for their alcohol and drug use while being in the home with their spouses, children, or extended family. What we heard from our clients was a level of desperation that they didn't even realize they had until they were forced to slow down, work less or engage remotely and move away from all activities they were accustomed to.

Many PIRs validated that the availability of virtual self-help meetings increased their engagement. Dr. Nitenson found that parents already in recovery fared better during this time, managed to maintain recovery in many cases, and turned to online self-help meetings and virtual therapy sessions. Rebecca, a working mother with two teenage children, embraced sobriety after a relapse during the pandemic and reported, "Zoom 12-step meetings saved my life. In many ways, the pandemic made getting sober easier." Nancy, a working mother of two children in their 20s, agreed, "Thank God for Zoom! If anything, my sobriety strengthened during the pandemic. I got to more meetings, talked to more sponsees on the phone and had more time for self-care." Tracie, a stay-at-home mother with school-age children, got sober during the pandemic with daily virtual meetings and found, "When I got sober, I had enough time during the day to devote to myself and my recovery. Self-care was a top priority, and my family allowed me the space and time I needed."

Some PIRs embraced social isolation more naturally and thrived. Claire, a working mother of two school-age boys, admits, "Honestly, as an anxious introvert prone to isolation and sloth, I loved it! I loved the proximity to my family and not having the pressures of any obligations." Sharon, working remotely without children in her home, shares, "That was an extremely isolating time, but it provided a space for quiet reflection, meditation, and personal growth. . . . I've never had such peace as I did during the quarantine." Chase, who is not currently living with his children, found that this time was "Good for me, it slowed me down so I could make better food and exercise decisions." Cathy, an author and mother to a school-age son, was one of few who enjoyed parenting during the pandemic, stating, "My son and I hiked together, and I didn't care about his grades and let him initiate his projects and, honestly, it was a blast. He was the right age of 12, so he didn't need me to oversee everything. He was making a series of videos that were hilarious." Natasha endorses, "It was tough at first without the physical connection, but I loved it. I really do not like leaving my home, so it was a gift for me to be able to work from home and pretty much do everything remotely."

Relapse Vulnerability

The transition to parenthood has different impacts on PIRs—for some, it can solidify their commitment to sobriety, while for others, it can exacerbate stressors and relapse potential. Either way, individuals in recovery from SUDs and their loved ones learn to live with the fear of potential relapse. Each individual needs to find unique relapse prevention strategies that work for them. However, they all agree that there is much at risk regarding the impact on their child(ren).

Many PIRs expressed that becoming a parent strengthened their commitment to sobriety for reasons such as increased accountability, consequences, and a sense of responsibility. Cathy endorses that "It has only been positive. As soon as my son was born, I felt this deeper commitment to my sobriety. Any lingering thoughts of maybe using someday became never using again. The fact that I am my son's only responsible, loving and tuned-in parent made me reach a new place of seriousness about being a sober person." She adds that while she had come close to relapsing before her son was born, she has never come close again. Cassie states, "I think having a child made me feel less vulnerable. . . . Even when my mind wanted relief from the stress of parenting, I knew that drinking was the worst option." Violet had a similar experience, stating, "The stress of becoming a parent definitely had me feeling more vulnerable to a relapse due to the overwhelming feelings that were brought on. But thinking of what that would do to his well-being made me less vulnerable as I played that tape forward." Chase, sober for 17 years, had three daughters before getting sober and one daughter afterward. He notes, "In the beginning, I felt pressure to stay sober and be present, and it motivated me to participate in my recovery to ensure I didn't relapse." Steve, sober for 16 years with a young son, has felt less vulnerable to relapse echoing, "Having someone else dependent on you and knowing that his life will end up very differently, challenged me to be more diligent."

Maggie, mother to a one-year-old son does not believe that having a child will keep her sober but instead attributes her increased stability to the fact that "My recovery program has changed, evolved and at the end of the day became more consistent since having a child." In contrast, Stacie has felt accountable to her family and wonders what changes in her recovery an empty nest may bring. "They play a part in helping me stay sober, especially when I remember the pain and despair that losing custody of my oldest son caused," she explains. Jackie notes, "My life shifted drastically when becoming a parent but I did not feel more or less vulnerable to relapse. It was more that the stakes of relapse became greater." Tracie became sober when her daughters were 11 and 13 and found, "Parenting sober is one of the greatest gifts in my life today. It's exponentially easier to parent sober than it was to parent drunk, hungover and in a constant cycle of shame, guilt and physical sickness."

Some PIRs struggled with increased vulnerability or an actual relapse. Joan, who got sober during her oldest daughter's first year, admits that "Trying to navigate through parenting when my sobriety was as new as my parenting definitely made me more vulnerable." Gina, sober for seven years, reveals, "I had a relapse after my son was 18 months old. . . . When I got sober again, I felt as though being a parent positively reinforced my recovery because I had something tangible to motivate me to get my shit together. During the relapse, I felt that I had 'space' (from parenting), and that changed when I got sober. However, we stay sober by putting our recovery first." She explains how this relapse led her to live a more balanced life and "humbled me that I had not 'figured it out' and has allowed me to stay in a healthier place." Evelyn became sober after her children were born but then relapsed ten years later. She reveals that her relapse led her toward a path of ongoing growth:

> It was only after my relapse and more work on myself, my inner narrative, and my boundaries that I was able to stop feeling debilitating shame as a parent. Now, I realize that everything we went through has created a stronger bond based on truth, no matter what, and the concept that we aren't defined by our mistakes or missteps but by how we respond to them is a cornerstone of my sober parenting. That, and that asking for help is an act of courage, not weakness. . . . After I got sober, I felt very vulnerable as a parent because the stresses of raising young kids was one of the main triggers for me. So, until I had a good amount of sobriety under my belt, I needed a good support system of other recovering people to help me navigate those vulnerable parenting feelings.

Parent Recovery Wisdom

PIRs and addiction treatment professionals highlight the following strategies and ideas for coping with various hard times. PIRs share how their recovery has been a source of strength during these times as well as coping strategies they have utilized to adapt to significant stressors and changes. Some are listed exactly as stated by the PIRs to capture their tone and message. While many reported a belief in some form of a higher power, that is not necessary to remain sober or to cope with difficulties. The following suggestions are meant to provide options and are not intended to be used in their entirety.

Recovery as a Source of Strength

- "I sometimes feel bad for people not in recovery. Anytime I have something I need to process or talk about, I have a list of people from meetings that I can call to talk to. Or if I'm feeling off, I can just get to a meeting, which always helps me feel at least a little bit better." —Stacie

- "Utilizing the 12-step principles has drastically changed my life. In difficult times, I default immediately to the steps and what I have learned and apply what I think is necessary." —Violet
- "I know what my resources are and have turned to them in the most difficult times." —Sharon
- "Do not 'put your kid first' above the things you have to do for yourself to stay sober and spiritually fit—you will just burn out, become resentful, feel like a victim, and feel completely out of touch with the positive feelings and reasons for having a family in the first place." —Natasha
- "In recovery, I learned to pray and invite my Higher Power in during the day. So, when difficult times come around, I invite it in as much as possible. This helps me get out of my own thinking, which tends to be negative and unhelpful. I'm also always looking at what my part in the difficult time is, and what I need to change (if anything)." —Nancy
- "I got back to the term powerless and that when you truly accept that you are powerless over everything except your own actions, it makes life much more manageable. I wouldn't have that if it weren't for my own recovery. Super grateful for that." —Maggie
- "Perspective of acceptance and viewing things as a set of conditions or a situation rather than being victimized by life." —David
- "So many times, my recovery has carried me through stressful times. The tools I learned in recovery help with everything. No matter how hard it gets, I know that drinking would make it so much worse. So, even when things are really hard, this knowledge keeps me hanging on. Also, when my kids struggle, they look to my recovery as a source of hope and inspiration—something I totally didn't expect would ever happen." —Evelyn

Coping Strategies for Hard Times

- Reach out to others for support, and be vulnerable.
- Work hard when things are good, don't wait for the struggle to happen before you start doing the work.

- Do NOT try to do it all.
- Maintain routine and structure, especially during stressful times.
- PAUSE.
- Practice grounding skills, such as listing what your five senses are experiencing or making a slight shift in each of them.
- Have a support system in place.
- Give yourself grace.
- Deal with issues in real time instead of avoiding them.
- Give yourself personal "time-outs."
- "Get out of the problem and into the solution."
- Take the time to pray and meditate.
- Change your environment by going outside or even into a different room.
- "A problem shared is a problem halved."
- Get out of your house and meet up with others who can offer valuable support.
- Prioritize yourself, even if you have to use this challenging time as the reason.
- Use a God box: write down the problem you want to turn over to your higher power and then place that paper into a designated container in order to "let go."
- Be honest that you are having a hard time.
- Seek spiritual or religious connection.
- Try to find meaning in the mess.

Personal Journal Entries

Throughout my recovery, many blessings, as well as difficult times, have come my way. For the first ten years of sobriety, when I was stressed or angry, I was susceptible to alcohol cravings. However, I recognized that was my "addiction talking" and I worked to ignore it. I allowed myself to feel, process, and vent about my emotions so that I could then move past them or the situation. Recovery has trained me to turn toward spiritual solutions for human problems to lessen my need for control. While I may kick and scream before I surrender—stepping away, viewing the larger picture, engaging supports, and turning the situation over to my Higher Power has become a habit. I also have a community of loved ones and sober peers who have supported me through my darkest times. The longer I am in recovery, the more faith I have in getting to the other side of the river, even when I cannot see the stepping stones.

October 17, 2017—Eve, six years old

There are times when I lay all alone in my bed,
And I feel a slight emptiness and fear in my head.
We are never alone, and in God we must trust—
We battle our minds, while there is always the divine.
Though you feel so afraid, the plan will be fine—
Just follow along, for this is destiny's ride.
Wherever you go, whatever you do—
You are existing with God, which makes two.

7

Staying Sane

Recovery from Mental Health Conditions

"They go hand in hand. The one led to the other."

—Joan, alcohol use disorder and bipolar disorder

A CRUCIAL ASPECT OF HEALING for many PIRs surrounds their mental health. While some individuals with SUDs have medical or other life situations to deal with, none co-occurs as frequently as mental illness. In fact, SUD and mental health issues can become so intertwined that this may obscure what is being treated in self-help and treatment programs. Therefore, understanding the similarities and differences can be life-changing and advantageous in how best to recover from both.

Co-Occurring Disorders

Co-occurring disorders refers to when an individual meets the criteria for one or more SUD(s) *and* one or more mental health condition(s). This can also be referred to as dual diagnosis. Some individuals are unaware that they have an underlying mental health condition until they become sober. In contrast, others minimize their substance use because their intention is to relieve their psychological symptoms. According to the National Survey on Drug Use and Health, half of all individuals with SUDs also have co-occurring "mild to moderate" mental illness—which amounts to over 17 million U.S. adults. Additionally, 5.7 million individuals have "serious mental illness" and a co-occurring SUD.[1] There is also a correlation between mental illness leading to SUDs, and SUDs contributing to the development or progression of mental illness.

In the general U.S. population, 52.9 million people, or 21 percent, have a diagnosed mental health condition. When surveyed, 17.9 percent of the control group of parents not in recovery reported a diagnosed mental health condition, 7.1 percent identified mental health symptoms without a diagnosis, and 75 percent reported not having mental health issues—relatively close to the national findings. In contrast, about half of the PIRs interviewed acknowledged having at least one co-occurring mental health diagnosis—also in keeping with the national findings. While mental health issues lead to a greater vulnerability for an SUD, 35 million individuals with mental health conditions did not develop one.[2] So, what makes a person more vulnerable to crossing the line of substance use into an SUD?

- *Genetics*: There is a 38–80 percent heritability rate of SUDs specific to the substance used and from a first-degree relative (see chapter 3).
- *Adverse childhood experiences (ACE) or post-traumatic stress disorder (PTSD)*: 46.4 percent of individuals with lifetime PTSD also met the criteria for SUD.[3]
- *Attention-deficit hyperactivity disorder (ADHD)*: Approximately 15 percent of adolescents and young adults with ADHD have a comorbid SUD, while 11 percent of individuals with an SUD also meet the criteria for ADHD. Both conditions have been described as disorders of disinhibition, suggesting a shared underlying vulnerability. Additionally, features of ADHD, such as impulsivity, may increase the risk of initiating substance use.[4]
- *Age of first use*:
    - Among those who first tried alcohol at age 14 or younger, 15.4 percent were diagnosed with an alcohol use disorder—notably higher than the 3.8 percent who started drinking at age 18 or older.[5, 6]
    - Among those who first tried marijuana at age 14 or younger, 11.5 percent were diagnosed with an SUD—notably higher than the 2.6 percent who first used marijuana at age 18 or older.[7]
    - This likelihood drops by 4 percent–5 percent for each year the start of substance use is delayed.[8, 9]

   - 74 percent of individuals ages 18–30 admitted for treatment reported starting alcohol or drug use at age 17 or younger—particularly for alcohol and marijuana usage. The age of onset for opiates was less telling, demonstrating how quickly dependence can occur at any age.[10]

- *Preexisting mental health diagnoses*: Anxiety disorders, depression, bipolar disorder, psychotic disorders, and several personality disorders are most commonly associated with co-occurring SUDs.[11]

When PIRs become sober, they may continue to struggle with mental health issues that either initially surfaced at that time or had been previously diagnosed or present. In other words, when the substance(s) is removed, active mental illness symptoms tend to surface. This may lead to physical and psychological dysregulation in sobriety—which can feel like negative reinforcement for making the healthy choice to get sober. Stacie, sober for 11 years since age 24, has been diagnosed with ADHD, depression, and anxiety. She describes how getting sober with ongoing mental health challenges has impacted her. "I struggle the most with ADHD, particularly when I hear about people in recovery without it who are able to keep their house clean and stay organized now that they are sober. I tend to compare myself to them because I am almost as messy and unorganized sober as I was in active addiction. ADHD can come with a lot of guilt and shame, which were my biggest triggers in addiction. It makes me feel like a bad parent when I forget small details. Many people do these things when using substances, but I do them in recovery, too!"

Many individuals are unaware of the connection between their mental health symptoms and delayed emotional development until they gain clarity from recovery. Jake, sober for 12 years since age 28, admits that as a result of his substance use, he had not learned ways to manage an anxiety disorder and ADHD. "I did not have any coping skills and was developmentally stunted." David, sober for 19 years since age 28 and diagnosed with PTSD, highlights, "Self-medication was no longer an option, so the mental health conditions became more glaring. . . . I would feel something and then reach to escape. Ultimately, I stunted that growth or the development of coping and solutions." Cassie, sober for 15 years since age 29, explains, "Looking back, I can see how they were interrelated. I certainly did not like the way anxiety made me feel, and I'm sure I used substances to try and self-treat. Alcohol definitely helped with social anxiety. I also wonder now if having ADHD didn't play into it as well. I wasn't diagnosed until later in life after I was sober, and when my doctor said I had it, my life made more sense."

Others were more aware of their need to self-medicate (see chapter 5) and of the role substances played until using became life-threatening. Cathy, sober for 23 years since age 32, reveals, "I felt like I couldn't be in my skin. I was suicidal because of the depression and anxiety and massively self-medicated. When I found heroin, I really felt like it was the only way I could stand to be alive. I am very grateful that I'm no longer suffering from the debilitating depression that almost killed me." Steve, sober for 16 years since age 23, recognized that "Trauma and PTSD were driving a lot of pain internally, and substances relieved it." Violet, sober for 18 years since age 20, emphasizes, "I truly believe I self-medicated to deal with my trauma and mental health."

Some PIRs recognized the interplay between SUD and mental health issues. Jackie, sober for 14 years since age 24, has periods of low mood and anxiety and explains, "When I'm using, my mental health suffers. When I remove drugs and alcohol, I'm able to regain functioning as a member of society." Chris, sober for 16 years since age 24, identifies that "They play off each other. Depression and anxiety are all part of 'Chris's version of substance use and mental health.'"

Mental Health Impact of Parenting

Having children has positive and negative effects on *all* parents. The impact, however, differs from parent to parent based on endless variables, which may include the temperament of the baby, access to childcare, socioeconomic status, preexisting mental health issues, parent's personality, marital status, and many others. While mothers having newly diagnosed perinatal and postpartum mood symptoms is often discussed, we hear less frequently about the impact of becoming a parent on those with preexisting mental health issues.

For some PIRs with preexisting mental health issues, postpartum mood symptoms can be hard to recognize. Cassie shares, "My anxiety was exacerbated. I had postpartum depression and refused to acknowledge it because I figured that my attendance at my self-help program was out of whack and I was just overtired. I suffered for way too long when there was help from a trained medical professional available." She also recognizes being faced with new challenges as her oldest son becomes a teenager and explains, "I also have had to work on strategies for ADHD as I am finding my symptoms get worse as my son has more activities on his plate."

Some PIRs have positive shifts in their mental health after having a child. Cathy notes, "I think it's made me stronger and happier. I feel more joy now. I am weepy with it sometimes. In the 15 years since he's been here, I've had no serious dips or relapses of depression at all. Sometimes the anxiety is bad, but that's more tolerable than clinical depression, and it goes away. My son brings me so much joy." Douglas, sober for 14 years since age 28, describes that having his son has created a "bond and love that has paid dividends for mental health."

Other PIRs have found that parenting adds additional strain to their mental health issues. Chris shares, "I cycle into a version of emotional instability every 18 months or so since having kids. It messes with my rhythms." Joan noted that the hormone shifts exacerbated her mood symptoms notably. Jackie, sober for 14 years since age 24 has found that "The mental load of being a parent can increase stress and irritability for me because it feels like so many decisions and so much information to hold. As a mother, I typically end up carrying the mental load of scheduling appointments, signing children up for activities, navigating family responsibilities, and even the mundane things like buying new socks and underwear." Steve is parenting an infant and reports, "My anxiety has been worse after becoming a parent and I see it play out more."

Other PIRs had a more neutral response to the impact of parenting and their baseline mood symptoms. Nancy, sober for 31 years since age 21, reflects, "The responsibility of raising two human beings is pretty intense. The combination of their struggles, my personal struggles, and how to continue to move together as a family unit is A LOT. But I would say that my mental health is not better or worse because of parenting."

Several PIRs reveal that they have become more motivated to get help for their mental health symptoms since becoming parents. David explains that parenting "made it more important. When I feel an occurrence, I deal with it immediately." Stacie endorses, "It has forced me to get help more quickly since my mental health directly affects my children."

PIRs have shared how becoming a parent has, for the most part, strengthened their recovery resolve. They also noted challenges regarding self-care, work/life balance, and time management. PIRs with mental health conditions have additional factors to contend with. Three of the most significant factors addressed by PIRs or not recognized at the time as impacting their mental health are sleep , trauma histories, and social anxiety.

Sleep

Adequate sleep is a standard clinical recommendation for those with mental health issues. However, some form of sleep deprivation is almost unavoidable when raising infants and even older children. A "Children and Sleep" poll by the National Sleep Foundation found that parents of children two months and younger slept, on average, 6.2 hours during the night, and this improved only slightly to 6.8 hours for parents of children ten years and older.[12] While interrupted and unpredictable sleep and early rising occur for different reasons at varying ages, the toll it takes on parents can be severe. Jennifer Senior, in her book *All Joy and No Fun: The Paradox of Modern Parenting*, summarizes sleep research, stating, "No matter what study they're consulting, though, most researchers agree that the sleep patterns of new parents are fragmented, unpredictable, and just plain rotten, failing to do the one thing we love most about sleep, which is to restore the body and mind." Some research compares the impact of brief periods of sleep deprivation to consuming excess alcohol.[13]

Sleep experts indicate that there are three different responses to prolonged sleep loss: those who handle it "fairly well," those who "sort of fall apart," and those who respond "catastrophically." However, most first-time parents are not aware of what their response may be until after the baby arrives.[14] Additionally, even small decreases in sleep impact parents' mental health. Findings about the first year after birth suggest that new and established parents who can get the recommended amount of sleep of seven or more hours per night may experience positive mental health effects.[15] Sleep deprivation can negatively affect individuals with preexisting mental illness, and not getting enough quality sleep can increase the risk of mental health disorders. While insomnia can be a symptom of psychiatric disorders, sleep problems can exacerbate mental health problems, including depression, anxiety, and suicidal ideation.[16] Violet describes the impact of sleep deprivation as a PIR with preexisting mental health conditions, explaining, "It wasn't until I had children and had significant postpartum issues with my first child that my mood symptoms exacerbated to an inability to function. The depression and anxiety that came from my becoming a new mother and having little sleep worsened my condition . . . sleep deprivation felt like torture at times. Especially with my second child, as she was a colicky baby and cried a lot and would wake up 4 to 5 times a night. My work and emotional state suffered, and I was more irritable and impatient with my oldest." Alex, sober for 12 years since age 31, recalls that sleep deprivation had a secondary effect in that "It could be really stressful on my marriage and other relationships that I had in my life along with not being able to continually physically take care of myself with a good self-care routine." Stacie agreed, stating, "I think the lack of sleep definitely made me more restless, irritable and discontented. I also went to fewer meetings because I was too tired to go anywhere. I was constantly in a state of 'just getting by.'"

Trauma

The impact of trauma manifests uniquely—even among those who have experienced the same event or situation. Situational stress, acute stress disorder, and post-traumatic stress disorder (PTSD) can result from traumatic events. While not everyone will develop PTSD, these events rewire the mind and imprint within the body. The book *The Body Keeps the Score*, by Bessel van der Kolk, sheds light on how traumatic experiences can leave enduring impacts on individuals, leading to a range of physical, emotional, and psychological challenges. He delves into the neuroscience of trauma, revealing how it alters brain structures and disrupts normal functioning.[17]

Some PIRs with a trauma history were in remission before having a child. The parenting role can lead to primal responses, particularly for those with adverse childhood experiences. These patterns can manifest as overprotection, overstimulation, anger, rescuing, avoidance, and hypervigilance. Alex has noticed, "I react sometimes due to past trauma and have codependency and a savior complex, especially with my wife. I can be over-the-top reactionary and protective of the family. I am aware that if I react in certain ways it would hurt my family." Other PIRs recognized that they were more protective and cautious in how they related to their children as a result of their own traumatic childhoods. Margo Friedman, LPC, LADC, a therapist in private practice, points out the importance of psychoeducation in the recovery process related to trauma: "There can be great progress made if the individual understands the relationship between their addiction and mental illness. I have found that a majority of my clients have had traumatic events that led them to seek alcohol and/or drugs to self-medicate and that once this is identified, the patient's level of shame seems to decrease. There is then greater willingness to work on their mental health and maintain sobriety."

Social Anxiety

The self-medication theory (discussed in chapter 5) finds that individuals with SUDs are drawn to substance(s) that provide some form of relief for them. For individuals who have social anxiety, shyness, or struggle to pick up on social cues—alcohol can feel like a magical cure and is so often available at social events. Alcohol, in particular, has often been referred to as "the social lubricant" and "liquid courage" for a reason. This central nervous system depressant lowers blood pressure, heart rate, brain activity, and respiratory rate—therefore decreasing stress and anxiety levels. Research indicates that individuals with social anxiety, in particular, are also at an increased risk for developing AUD. Social anxiety disorder (SAD) is a mental health diagnosis characterized by intense fear and stress in social situations. It includes worries such as being judged or embarrassed and can impact their ability to communicate effectively. Specifically, SAD was the only one of the seven anxiety disorders that predicted some amount of causation with an AUD 10 years later.[18] Further validation of the self-medication theory for these individuals as well as a reason to obtain treatment for SAD before it increases chances of developing an AUD.

When individuals with SAD become sober, it can add another layer of difficulty in forming new peer supports and navigating social situations. While many PIRs reported that they may have felt a level of discomfort socializing without substances, those with SAD have distress that more often leads them to avoid interactions. Stacie felt the most challenging aspect of socializing as a PIR involved having social anxiety. Attending

12-step meetings, public speaking, and "connecting with sober peers provided exposure to gradually increase her ease and confidence." However, she still feels she stands out among other parents because "I am viewed as uptight sometimes when other parents are drinking and I am not." SAD can lead PIRs to be quieter and more reserved, which can be misinterpreted by other parents who may be more outgoing while drinking. Additionally, if not properly addressed or treated, it can lead them to be more vulnerable to relapse socially.

Integrated Treatment

Behavioral health treatment in the United States is frequently compartmentalized to focus on either SUDs or mental health conditions. Research indicates that the conditions should be treated concurrently for those with co-occurring disorders. Unfortunately, of the 17 million individuals with co-occurring disorders, only 5.7 percent or 960,000 individuals received both substance use and mental health services simultaneously. Of the 5.7 million individuals with "severe mental illness" and SUD, only 9.3 percent or 529,000 received appropriate integrated treatment.[19]

Originally, individuals received sequential treatment—the SUD was addressed first, and once stabilized, the mental health condition was treated. An advantage can be that the most acute condition is treated first—but the second condition may not receive adequate care. When individuals are in extreme distress from an untreated mental health condition in early sobriety, it can also lead them to relapse—which emphasizes the need to address these conditions simultaneously. SUD treatment programs also tend to focus on addiction-related topics, while mental health treatment programs may not address substance use.

As a result of research and clinical outcomes, the past two decades have seen a shift toward integrated treatment. Dr. Roger Weiss and Dr. Hilary Connery, in their book, *Integrated Group Therapy for Bipolar Disorder and Substance Abuse*, developed an evidence-based curriculum for dual diagnosis treatment.[20] This modality is applicable to most mental health conditions. Because of the reciprocal dynamic between SUDs and mental illness, a core concept is considering and treating the two as *one* condition. However, this can be challenging with segmented treatment. It is possible for treatment programs and clinicians with expertise to guide clients in obtaining the proper integrated care.

The concept of integrated treatment itself can be helpful for PIRs in terms of recognizing the necessity of recovery from both conditions. When individuals self-medicate for a mental health issue or extreme emotions, compartmentalization occurs within their psyche. Most individuals identify more as having either an SUD or a mental health condition—or view one as primary. While this may be true, this treatment emphasizes not favoring one condition above the other. Each condition needs to be addressed equally; if one is neglected, it can lead to suffering and possibly relapse. PIRs shared how they have addressed their mental health in addition to their SUD recovery. They point out that psychoeducation through books and other resources has been a great help for their mental health recovery. Cassie shares, "I currently have an ongoing relationship with a therapist whom I see about every three weeks. Exercise and eating healthy are important and make a difference when I make time to work them into my schedule. Meditation has also been important, and I need both a recovery program and a mental health program to support me to feel healthy and happy." Jackie describes her journey, stating, "The longer I have remained sober and reconnected with myself, the more I have been able to resolve trauma that I have carried with me. I have seen therapists, gone to reiki providers, attended 12-step meetings, and created a self-care plan that has kept my mental health in a consistently good place." Stacie describes the specific plan she has developed for her different mental health conditions: "For ADHD, it is mostly adjusting my expectations, educating my family, and coming up with systems for productivity that work with instead of against it. For anxiety and depression, meditation has helped me tremendously, as well as getting outside more, especially for depression. For anxiety, I usually take it as a hint from my body to get up and do something physical—clean, go for a walk, get chores done." Violet has dedicated much time in her recovery to healing from past trauma and explains that she engages in "self-care, exercise, sees a psychiatrist, trauma therapy, transcranial magnetic stimulations and takes medication."

While seeking integrated treatment is beneficial, it can be detrimental when group members in SUD self-help programs claim that those groups can treat mental health issues. Or to the contrary, group members discourage members from pursuing mental health treatment because they believe the program can treat all conditions. Group members in any of these SUD self-help groups should not be taking on the role of a therapist or physician in talking with group members about their mental health treatment choices. Nancy explains how this type of interference impacted her, "I have a hard time listening to mental health advice in SUD self-help meetings. It is usually made by people who do not exhibit similar symptoms to mine and, therefore, is not helpful. Such advice tends to be to avoid taking medication, or 'just work the program,' which is also not useful and borders on irresponsible." Violet had an unfortunate experience of receiving medical advice from an unqualified group member, revealing, "Sadly, in my self-help program, I was misguided to not take any medication in recovery. I educated myself and spoke with professionals, and I will say there are individuals in self-help programs who have no room to discuss mental health medications with anyone."

Jennifer Barba, LCSW, describes firsthand the intricacies of working with clients with co-occurring disorders, explaining,

> Engaging and maintaining compliance with treatment can be particularly demanding for clients grappling with both addiction and mental health issues. I implement motivational techniques, build strong therapeutic alliances and identify barriers to the engagement process. With comprehensive strategies, I support clients in navigating their mental health symptoms, fostering motivation, and managing addiction-related cravings. To ensure integrated and seamless care, I collaborate closely with mental health professionals, addiction specialists and other healthcare providers. Coordinating efforts across treatment settings, I ensure effective communication, shared treatment planning and holistic support for my clients.

Molly Ashcroft, CADC, ICADC adds that some SUD specialists struggle to transition their treatment modalities to accommodate mental health symptoms, explaining, "Many providers who are familiar with SUDs are accustomed to treating addiction through a certain lens that can include motivational interviewing, behavior modification and 12-step support among others. When treating an individual with an additional diagnosis such as a personality disorder or mood disorder along with a substance use disorder, the way we treat the individual needs to shift." It is also essential that PIRs with mental health issues understand the interplay between these symptoms. Liz Modugno, LCSW, LADC, emphasizes, "Another challenge is working with a client to learn how both the addiction and mental health symptoms impact each other. Sometimes it can feel like 'whack-a-mole' to clients who might say, 'I stopped drinking, but now I am really anxious and have no coping skills besides drinking.' Understanding that addiction and mental health cannot be treated separately is important."

Emotional Sobriety

The typical association with "sobriety" is physical abstinence from a substance. Once individuals have achieved physical sobriety it is their minds, bodies, and emotions that remain. There is no longer an escape or way to "check out" with substances. Emotional sobriety may take time to address and may not initially be a clear need.

The term "emotional sobriety" originated from Bill Wilson, the founder of Alcoholics Anonymous, in a letter he wrote to a friend who was struggling with depression, stating, "I think that many oldsters who have put our A.A. 'booze cure' to severe but successful tests still find they often lack emotional sobriety. Perhaps they will be the spearhead for the next major development in A.A., the development of much more real maturity and balance (which is to say, humility) in our relations with ourselves, with our fellows, and with God." He writes that while individuals may have used A.A. for their alcoholism, some may still experience difficulty with emotions and overall life balance.[21] Other A.A. literature has suggested that individuals should not hesitate to seek help for mental health issues.

Through the years, the term emotional sobriety has been used beyond 12-step programs in various contexts. In her book, *Emotional Sobriety: From Relationship Trauma to Resilience and Balance*, Tian Dayton discusses this concept as it relates to mind and body healing from the use of substances in self-medicating symptoms of depression, anxiety, and relationship trauma. She defines emotional sobriety as recovery that "encompasses our ability to live with balance and maturity. It means that we have learned how to keep our emotions, thoughts, and actions within a balanced range. Our thinking, feeling, and behavior are reasonably congruent and we're not ruled or held captive by any one part of us."[22] This term can apply to PIRs with emotional issues and to those with diagnosable mental health conditions. Emotional sobriety can be likened to mental health recovery. In fact, according to the Substance Abuse and Mental Health Services Administration (SAMHSA), 66.5 percent of individuals with mental health issues consider themselves to be "in recovery." This is comparable to the 72.2 percent of adults who have *ever* had an SUD who consider themselves "in recovery."[23]

It can be helpful for PIRs to understand signs of emotional sobriety in order to identify possible areas of growth. These can include the ability to:

- Regulate emotions
- Manage mood symptoms
- Minimize the use of other addictive or compulsive behaviors (e.g., food, spending, sex)
- Hold a healthy perspective on life circumstances
- Bring their mind into the present moment
- Moderate activity levels
- Maintain social and intimate connections
- Take responsibility for actions and avoid falling into a victim role
- Own and process emotions
- Have resiliency in returning to a balanced mental and physical state.[24]

Obtaining emotional sobriety is a process that continues to "peel back the layers of the onion" throughout an individual's recovery. It is not something that is achieved and then completed. Joe, sober for 23 years since age 27, says, "If we are not in a stable place with our emotions, that can have a negative impact on our ability to parent." He further outlines his emotional sobriety journey, stating, "As the years have gone by, I have needed to do different things to maintain my emotional sobriety. In the beginning, the 12 steps and helping other alcoholics were enough. Then I needed to address my trauma at about eight years in. After that, I needed to go deeper and sought other spiritual practices—meditation and breathwork have been a huge help. I've also needed to move physically. Brazilian jiujitsu and working out have been instrumental in my overall well-being. In the beginning, it was about engaging in different spiritual and self-care practices, and now it's a way of life." Stacie explains that recovery has allowed her to seek out emotional sobriety, describing, "During active addiction, I would do the bare minimum to get by as a mother with depression." She adds that recovery has taught her to reach out for help for her mental health without an added layer of shame.

Parent Recovery Wisdom

The following strategies are from PIRs themselves and addiction treatment professionals. These approaches focus on mental health recovery and integrated suggestions for recovery from co-occurring disorders. Some are listed exactly as stated by the PIRs to capture their tone and message. The following suggestions are meant to provide options and are not intended to be used in their entirety.

Mental Health Recovery

Coping strategies for SUD and mental health can have some overlap. The difference lies in how these skills are targeted.

- Utilize applicable SUD recovery principles for mental health recovery.
- Address underlying or resulting trauma, and seek ongoing care.
- Know that you are not alone and work to address shame.
- Engage in sleep hygiene practices.
- Be prepared for hard times when addressing underlying issues.
- Consider how your diet is impacting your mood.
- Give your mind time to heal.
- Be a role model in healthy brain wellness for your children.
- Be honest with yourself about how you are feeling in sobriety.
- Learn about mental health conditions.
- Share in self-help groups and with others about your mental health challenges and successes—it can be healing for everyone.
- Work on cognitive behavioral therapy (CBT) concepts of recognizing, identifying, and challenging thought distortions (mind reading, magnification, black and white thinking, etc.).

- Attempt to detach from stuck thought patterns. (reading recommendation: "The Power of Now," chapter 1 of *You Are Not Your Mind*).[25]
- Seek out specialized evidence-based clinical support for mental health that may include:
    - PTSD: seeking safety, eye movement desensitization, and reprocessing (EMDR)
    - Obsessive-compulsive disorder: exposure and response prevention, acceptance and commitment therapy
    - Anxiety: cognitive-behavioral therapy, exposure hierarchies, mindfulness, meditation practice
    - Depression, bipolar disorder: mindfulness-based cognitive therapy, self-compassion practice, cognitive-behavioral therapy, integrated group therapy
    - Personality disorders: dialectical behavioral therapy, mentalization-based approaches

Integrated Recovery

- Find a therapist who can address and educate you about co-occurring disorders.
- Create a treatment plan that includes support for *both* your SUD and mental health conditions.
- Notice which condition you tend to identify with, and focus on the one you tend to ignore.
- Shop around for a therapist with whom you feel safe and can connect with.
- Obtain a medication management assessment, if clinically appropriate.
- Choose treatment professionals who can work as a team to coordinate care.
- Explore alternative treatment approaches that respect sobriety.
- Note that mental health diagnoses can shift from early sobriety and onward as brain chemistry and post-acute withdrawal symptoms subside.

- Complete a "symptom map" to help you identify and separate your SUD and mental health symptoms:

  1. What people activate my SUD and mental health symptoms?
  2. What places or environments activate my SUD and mental health symptoms?
  3. What people, times of day, days of the week, or months of the year trigger my SUD or mental health symptoms?
  4. What other things impact my SUD or mental health condition? Am I *H*ungry, *A*ngry, *L*onely, *T*ired, or *S*ick (HALTS)?
  5. What positive or negative emotions do I notice right before I am going to engage in (this SUD behavior) or before I start to feel (mental health symptoms/diagnosis)?
  6. What thoughts do I have before engaging in (SUD behavior) or right before I feel (mental health symptoms)?
  7. What parts of my SUD and mental health condition fit together? For example, when I am depressed, do I drink, gamble, or do both? When I drink, do I feel depressed, anxious, or both the next day?
  8. What coping skills help when I want to (SUD behavior) or feel (mental health symptoms)?
  9. Who can I call when I want to (SUD behavior) or feel (mental health symptoms)?
  10. Where can I go when I want to (SUD behavior) or feel (mental health symptoms)?

Personal Journal Entries

May 26, 2013—Eve, 18 months old

I am being forced into submission to let go of control and reassurance. Therefore, I am more aware and appreciative of the moment. Fear still lingers in the background, but I am trying to focus on faith that God will take care of me—and has a plan.

May 27, 2013

Hope—in the form of reassurance from my therapist—that I will be okay, that I am experiencing a mental health episode. It is a relief that she has labeled it and reassured me that I will get through it. I have started a new medication to help manage the anxiety. I am grateful for medication because it allows me to be the person I am meant to be without mental health barriers.

Gratitude: I feel hope, medication, Eve's laughter and joy, cuddling with Eve and reading books.

It is so scary to see your life in front of you and be almost unable to live it because of anxiety. It is as though you can feel the normalcy, but then it slips through your hands. When prayer and trying to connect with your Higher Power do not work—you feel alone. But God will be waiting for me on the other side, He always is. My leaps of faith are without connection—that is why they are a leap.

June 9, 2013

Gratitude: Ocean, sun, boat, family, nature, healing, Eve sleeping on the boat—so cute.

I am slowly trying to rebuild trust in my mind and nervous system . . . I feel that my therapists are in support of helping me to be truly balanced and do not feel I should live in such (previous) distress. I am healing . . .

From Daily Reflections:

"My planting will require patience and my realizing that some flowers will be more perfect than others. Each stage of the petals unfolding can bring wonder and delight if I do not interfere or let my expectations override my acceptance—and this brings serenity."[26]

8

The "Dog Years"

Coping with the Most Challenging Stages

"Embracing motherhood has led me to be far more vulnerable, which mirrors my early recovery days. Early recovery was filled with so many emotions, which felt very familiar as I embraced motherhood. It has very much been a full circle moment for me to embrace a range of emotions, fears and joy. I have been much more open to sharing these experiences for support rather than keep my nose down and just 'grinding out.'"

—Maggie

EACH DEVELOPMENTAL PHASE of childrearing presents joys and obstacles for mothers and fathers, and much depends on the individual temperaments and constitutions of both the parent and the child. Intrinsic and extrinsic parenting traits can influence a PIR's experience of a particular stage. While some parents thrive during the infant stage, others connect more with tweens and teens. Fears may surface around genetic predisposition to SUDs, mental health, and keeping children safe. Time can drag on during the more difficult years, impacting PIRs' stability, emotional sobriety, and potentially increasing relapse vulnerability. In contrast, the easier years can increase PIRs' confidence, commitment to recovery, and resiliency.

Parenting Stages

Parents tend to share more about the blessings and joys of parenthood than they do about the challenges—leading listeners to assume they are not having difficulties. Not everyone feels comfortable expressing how lost they feel or asking questions of other parents. This can stem from gratitude for having their child(ren), societal expectations, knowing that many struggle to conceive or believing that having a hard time means they are not "good" parents. Some parents have a sense of shame and remain silent about their struggles. Jennifer Barba, LCSW, has observed that each parenting stage brings distinct joys and difficulties and that "The challenges faced by PIR clients vary depending on factors such as their temperament, the child's temperament and the specific dynamics within the family." Knowing that other parents have similar feelings can be liberating and comforting. The Pew Research Center found that 62 percent of parents report it has been "harder than expected," and 26 percent report it's been "much harder." This is especially true of mothers, 30 percent of whom say being a parent has been "a lot harder" than they expected, compared with 20 percent of fathers.[1]

There can also be a false assumption that other parents are experts on the subject and in sync with their life's purpose. In her book, *Mommy Doesn't Drink Here Anymore*, Rachel Brownell was falling apart as a mother of newborn twins, yet she did not want to share her pain with others, writing, "I'm coming unglued. And even though I'm thirty-three, I have very few close female friends who have kids, so I feel alone and untethered. I go to one of those 'Mommy and Me' support groups, but I'm much too afraid and proud to sully the happy get-together with the truth: I have no idea how to do this. I look around and think everyone else is happily married and delighted by motherhood."[2] Whatever the journey, PIRs interviewed expressed their raw feelings about parenting children of various ages, which may prevent others from feeling alone and cultivating more realistic expectations of themselves.

Another factor impacting PIRs is the age of their child(ren) when they become sober. Marilyn became sober when her children were preteens and found that this coincided with her own personal challenges. Joan, sober for ten years, does not remember her oldest daughter's first year as she was in active addiction and getting sober. The reality is that every stage has peaks and valleys and differing past and present scenarios that influence a parent's perception.

Pregnancy Stage

Pregnancy is experienced differently—some associate it with slowing down, nesting, and self-care, while others recall physical discomfort, mood fluctuations, and fear. Different trimesters may ease or increase particular psychological and physical symptoms as well. Prenatal hormones are powerful and impact each individual differently—some feel a sense of calm, while 15–21 percent have increased symptoms of anxiety and depression.[3, 4] Mood symptoms can be even more complicated when women suddenly stop using alcohol or substances, are medically advised to taper off certain psychotropic medications that may be unsafe during pregnancy or personally decide to stop taking psychotropic medications without medical supervision. Plus, information (both accurate and inaccurate) is so easily accessible on the internet that pregnant women can find new issues to be concerned about, and those who may not have been worried are given cause for panic.

Regardless of the experience, pregnancy lends itself to miraculous stories. In her book *The Soul Grind*, Jaydee Graham, MSSW, bravely reveals her traumatic childhood and battle with addiction. Her book concludes when she becomes unexpectedly pregnant, leading to an awakening. She realizes that her love for this unborn child trumps her need for substances and warrants a massive lifestyle change, writing,

> I knew that it may take a ton of healing, a ton of hard times, a ton of growing up and wising up and opening up and being healthy, but I was going to be it. This baby gave me this opportunity. The opportunity to be who I was intended to be. I might not have been worthy of this in my own eyes, for myself. But this baby was worth it and therefore, I could and would do and be that . . . I knew I had to get my life together and that might mean I needed it to break even harder and fuller. Then I could pick up the pieces and rid my life of those who no longer could be part of my life. But I had hope. And I had this baby.[5]

Claire, who got sober between the births of her four- and seven-year-old sons, also shares how motivating and life-changing pregnancy was, pointing out,

> I loved being pregnant for many reasons. The predominant one was that drinking was simply off the table. I didn't have the mental battle of "to drink or not to drink," which I always lost in the end. I had a reprieve from the embarrassment, shame, hangovers and self-loathing. But, like a good alcoholic, as soon as I stopped breastfeeding, it was off to the races. I remember feeling a little devastated and totally disappointed in myself. I drank for another six months before I quit for good. Having experienced sobriety through pregnancy showed me what my life could be like, and I wanted that again. In a way, my pregnancy saved me.

For others, the pregnancy experience was harder to navigate. Jessica Grose interviewed a diverse group of mothers for her book *Screaming on the Inside: The Unsustainability of American Motherhood.* She was shocked at how many women had pictured pregnancy through a magical lens of glowing and complete contentment. In contrast, they felt badly that they were not enjoying it as much as they had envisioned.[6] She also revealed her personal physical and mental health hurdles, explaining, "I went off antidepressants to conceive because I felt I needed to be as 'natural' as possible. I still don't know where I got this notion, except from the maternal expectations that had seeped into me through some kind of demented osmosis. The doctors around me didn't tell me I had to get off the medication, but they didn't stop me from going off it, either.[7] None of them told me the relapse rate for pregnant women who discontinue their antidepressants may be as high as 68 percent[8] . . . I found out I was pregnant on my second day of that shiny new job and I had about a week of grace before it all fell apart. I started vomiting uncontrollably, at least five times a day. . . . My depressive and anxious symptoms came roaring back shortly after I started throwing up."[9] Stacie, who got sober after having her first of three children, found the pregnancy and newborn stage stressful, stating, "I felt like my body was not my own, which triggered PTSD from sexual assaults during my addiction." Maggie, sober 15 years and before her toddler son's birth, spoke of the surrender necessary, "Being pregnant was the closest thing to the feeling of getting sober—powerlessness."

Newborn Stage (birth to age one)

Nothing can truly prepare parents for the paradigm shift of having a newborn—a paradox of wonder and overwhelm. Jennifer Senior, author of *All Joy and No Fun*, observes, "One day you are a paragon of self-determination, coming and going as you please; the next, you are a parent, laden with gear and unhooked from the rhythms of normal adult life. It's not an accident that the early years of parenting often register in studies as the least happy ones. They're the bunker years, short in the scheme of things but often endless-seeming in real-time."[10] While those in and out of recovery from an SUD have some common personality traits such as being self-centered, willful, and thrill-seeking—becoming a parent is the polar opposite of considering another's needs, lacking control and slowing down.

It is impossible to explore the newborn stage without considering the impact of postpartum hormones and mood symptoms. Many PIRs indicated that the newborn stage (followed by the tween and teenager stages) was the most challenging for various reasons, including lack of routine, boredom, relationship stress, sleep deprivation, fear, and constant infant needs. Parents not in recovery surveyed responded that the newborn and tween/teenager stages were the most difficult. The Pew Center Research found that parents with children five and under are likelier than those whose children are five or older to find parenting tiring and stressful; 57 percent of those with children five and under found being a parent tiring all or most of the time, compared with 39 percent of those whose youngest child is five to 12 years old, and 24 percent of those whose youngest child is a teenager. And while 35 percent of those with a child younger than five say parenting is stressful all or most of the time, about 25 percent of those whose children are five or older say the same.[11]

Postpartum mental health issues can be more likely for parents with preexisting mental health issues or they may occur randomly. CDC research shows that about one in eight women experience symptoms of postpartum depression. Additionally, the rate of depression diagnoses at delivery was seven times higher in 2015 than in 2000.[12] While the term "postpartum depression" is most often used, there is a spectrum of other perinatal (the period of pregnancy and one year following delivery) mental health conditions that can arise or be exacerbated—anxiety, obsessive-compulsive disorder, post-traumatic stress disorder, bipolar disorder, and psychosis. While medical professionals may conduct maternal screenings more often during the first six months to one year after birth, the onset of symptoms can be delayed. Symptoms can begin when oxytocin levels abruptly drop once breastfeeding ends, or it can be due to other biological and situational factors. Jill Griffin, LCSW, LADC, has observed, "The newborn stage can be so disorienting because it is uncharted territory, particularly for women and their hormonal fluctuations. I spend a lot of time helping women notice the drastic effect of their menstrual cycle or hormone levels on their mental health. It is important to have some awareness of what's going on in your physical body, which can affect your ability to show up and parent." Natasha, six years sober with a seven-month-old son, recalls that her birthing and immediate postpartum experience greatly impacted early motherhood, stating, "I had a C-section and spinal headaches and was in a lot of pain, and I couldn't parent the way I wanted to." However, once the pain subsided, she realized, "The most joyful time is now because he is active and sweet. I'll feel even better when we can sleep again because we'll be rested and able to show up as ourselves and fully soak up the experience instead of just living in survival mode." She also noted that the most significant stressor as a PIR has been taking opiate pain medication as prescribed following her C-section—a high-risk scenario for those in recovery from opiate use disorder. Nancy, sober for 31 years prior to having her now two adult children, recalls, "When the kids were babies, I was up two to three times a night. My wife suggested couples therapy, but I didn't understand why. When we were in therapy, she explained that I was moody, had unpredictable emotions and wasn't fun to be around. We realized that it was due to sleep deprivation. She then took on all the nighttime responsibilities, and I became a human again."

Men can also have mental health issues after the birth of their child. Research indicates that perinatal depression is evident in about 10 percent of men and is relatively higher three to six months after birth.[13] 4.1 percent to 16 percent of fathers exhibit anxiety disorder symptoms during the prenatal period and 2.4 percent to 18 percent during the postpartum period.[14] This may be due to actual hormonal changes that can include decreases in testosterone and an increase in cortisol and other hormones.[15] In addition, shifts in routine, sleep, and dynamics with their partner may all contribute. Chris reveals that he felt he had "lost my wife after the special time of pregnancy" and sought professional support. He learned that because of his wife's maternal instinct, "She can't consider your needs right now."

Few PIRs interviewed identified the first year of parenting as their preferred stage. However, many other parents prefer this stage to others. Dave, sober for 19 years, had two daughters when he was in active addiction and two boys after getting sober. He expresses that he has enjoyed each stage of development of his boys and attributes his ability to be present, this time, with maturity and fostering his emotional sobriety. Laura, sober for 38 years prior to having her now two grown sons, notes that her recovery "keeps me in the day and appreciating the little things. I love being a parent and enjoy each stage. All stages have stress, but when it comes down to it, as a parent, keeping them safe is the biggest challenge." Many PIRs expressed difficulties during this time. Some had difficulty with their ability to maintain their previously established recovery lifestyle (see chapter 1); they had found a sense of balance within their life domains and a newborn baby disrupted their ability to engage in enough self-care and recovery efforts. Liz Modugno, LCSW, LADC, observed, "These are very demanding years, and often there is difficulty and shame to put one's recovery first when a small child demands much time and attention. When a child becomes the center of attention, it is easy to become consumed with parenting and less involved in one's recovery. That's why family and spousal support can be so crucial. Putting recovery before your children sounds harsh, but without recovery, many will not be in their children's lives or the best parents they can be for their children."

Another factor can be the great anticipation of the arrival of a newborn; if the reality does not match the idealized vision, admitting disappointment can feel shameful. Additionally, many PIRs established a new sense of self when they got sober. Becoming a parent changes one's identity—which can be beneficial and earth-shattering. Jennifer Barba, LCSW, notes, "PIR clients may grapple with adjusting to the demands of caring for a baby, sleep deprivation, and navigating their new role as a parent." Jessica Valenti, in her book *Why Have Kids: A New Mom Explores the Truth About Parenting and Happiness*, interviewed a variety of mothers and found, "The overwhelming sentiment, however, was the feeling of a loss of self, the terrifying reality that their lives had been subsumed into the needs of their child."[16] Natasha explains, "His needs keep changing, and just when I get into a routine or become comfortable, he changes again." Cassie, mother of an eight-year-old and sober for 15 years, admits, "It was so much work with little reward. I had this colicky baby, and it was just hard. I felt *very* alone when my son was a baby. I was lugging him to places, such as meetings, because I did not have childcare." Chris, sober for 16 years with two young daughters, reflects on this time and that "I have gotten down on my hands and knees to pray to a God I did not believe in to make the baby stop crying." Valerie, sober for 24 years with two young sons, recalls, "The first years of my son's lives were very hard on me, and two of the biggest fights I have been in with my husband were during these times. I was so tired and did not ask for enough help." Maggie states that she struggled with the "reintegration to being a full-time working parent after maternity leave, which caused stress, uncertainty, guilt and fear if I was making the right decision. In addition, the lack of sleep the first year caused plenty of challenges on my mental health and not feeling like 'myself.'"

Toddler Stage (ages one to three)

Containing an infant may seem easy relative to the active crawling and walking of a toddler. Parents are on a new kind of alert as the child's mobility and curiosity take over. Ellie Schoenberger, founder and former host of the Bubble Hour recovery-focused podcast, describes the evolution that listeners have shared,

> The ability to be present for their children and families doesn't happen right away . . . I think as many of us numbed the boredom, irritation, insecurity and worry that comes with parenting with drugs and/or alcohol . . . learning to be present with *all* the emotions parenting brings, like the intense love, the fear of screwing up, the joyous moments, and the challenges didn't really feel like a blessing at first. But over time, the gift of presence and the ability to consistently show up for their families is the most common feedback I hear from recovering parents.

Jackie, sober for 14 years with a young son and tween daughter, was able to remain present enough to apply healthy coping skills and describes, "A child learning to be independent and finding their voice is such a wonderful thing to watch but also comes with its own challenges. During this stage, I found that I had to soothe my nervous system to manage the tantrums and power struggles with this toddler phase." She also felt this stage was lighter and easier for her than the transition to the tween years because "Life seemed simpler when they were babies and just giggled when they looked at me."

As their children start talking, parents may try reasoning and become frustrated when that approach is ineffective. Jennifer Senior writes, "Toddlers cannot appreciate, as an adult can, that when they're told to put their blocks away, they'll be able to resume playing with them later. . . . They want them now because now is where they live. Yet somehow mothers and fathers believe that if only they could convey the *logic* of their decisions, their young children would understand it."[17] Mark, sober for 19 years with three children, notes that "the irrational years of toddler life were tough for me personally" and also adds that there were a lot of dangers to protect children from, such as drowning, choking, and falling. Tracie, a stay-at-home mother, sober for two and a half years with 13- and 16-year-old daughters, found this stage hard because "So much energy goes into parenting young children, and it felt emotionally exhausting at times. It was my only job, so I felt that I had to be great and put in extra effort, many times ignoring my own needs." Stacie also observed this disconnect between parental logic and children's impulsive behavior, explaining, "They are old enough not to be considered completely helpless and innocent but also cannot process things the same way as an adult. It felt very emotionally volatile raising toddlers, both on my end and on their end. I wish I could have kept my cool more often." She also found that the chaos of this stage was "extremely triggering; I get overstimulated easily."

Many aspects of parenting toddlers and younger children are the complete opposite of substance use or active addiction. The concept of "flow" was introduced by Mihaly Csikszentmihalyi in his book *Flow: The Psychology of Optimal Experience*. He found that activities leading to a flow state fully engage individuals' attention and push their abilities.[18] Similar to athletes who describe being in the "zone," or "A state of being in which we are so engrossed in the task at hand—so fortified by our own sense of agency, of mastery—that we lose all sense of our surroundings, as though time has stopped."[19] Substance use may have been a shortcut for some PIRs in achieving this artificial flow state, and many in recovery seek activities that can recreate some of this feeling through extreme activities. Therefore, PIRs are experiencing the interruption in both natural or artificial flow states that they may be more apt to crave. To compensate, some have found healthier outlets such as work, exercise, nature, spiritual, or artistic pursuits. Parenting a toddler and a young child creates a ricochet between boredom and anxiety. Dr. Daniel Gilbert, a social psychologist, notes, "To the extent that we are not maximally happy when we're with young children, it could be that they're demanding things of us we find difficult to give. But it could also be that they're not demanding *that* much."[20] To this point, Brenda Wilhelmson, author of the memoir *Diary of an Alcoholic Housewife*, has had mothers contact her inquiring if she is still sober and "tell me that they're struggling with the boredom and grind of everyday life." These parents have a dire need to integrate interesting and stimulating activities into their everyday lives.

Young Child Stage (ages four to ten)

Young children are more aware of their surroundings and their parent's behaviors. This is also the time when their long-term memory is intact, and parents know, on some level, that these are the years when what they say and do matters on a deeper level. Even so, this stage appears to be easier for some parents to navigate than the earlier and later ages.

Chris has found that "I enjoyed ages four through eight the best. It's like everything is magic for them." Nancy found her most content years were after the toddler stage and up until the teenage stage, explaining, "We had so much fun! They loved us and shared their thoughts and feelings with us. It felt like we knew them so well. They would ask us for help. The emotional upheavals of toddlerhood were over, and we hadn't yet seen too much from the early teenage years." Violet, sober for 18 years with three children, found "Up until age five were the most challenging years for me because at those ages they demanded so much time and attention." She found a noticeable difference when her children turned six, pointing out, "I am enjoying the ages my kids are now because they are all independent." Jackie affirms, "Since my daughter entered school, many more social challenges and teaching opportunities have come up. I enjoy being able to have more mature conversations as she ages."

This stage can be challenging when PIRs are still working on their own emotional sobriety while trying to have patience and lead by example. It can also be a time when PIRs begin to read into their children's behaviors and overanalyze if they appear to have "addictive personalities." However, much of what may appear to be a flag is part of the normal childhood development at these ages. Stacie acknowledges, "Teaching emotional regulation when I don't have it completely down myself has been really hard."

Tweens, Teenager and Young Adult Stages (ages 11+)

Parents find the tween and older stages difficult to manage for many reasons. Research indicates that children may have more intense interactions and dynamics with the same-sex parent. They also may have a closer connection; when independence occurs, it can feel more personal and painful. Another issue in this stage is that parents may respond more strongly to their tweens and teenagers based on their own past experiences. Brené Brown, PhD, explains, "I think it's a lot easier to parent children before their struggles start to reflect your struggles. The first time our kids don't get a seat at the cool table, or they don't get asked out, or they get stood up—that is such a shame trigger."[21] Liz Modugno, a trauma specialist elaborates,

> Often parents who experienced difficulty, trauma or substance use and abuse at certain ages during their childhood, adolescence and teens become triggered when their child enters into that age or stage of their lives. Many people struggle to raise tweens and teenagers because that may have been when addictive behaviors started to form for the PIR and the consequences and traumas of addiction started to happen. Trauma symptoms, shame, guilt and fear can play out for a PIR when their child starts to display similar patterns and behaviors at those same ages.

Jackie anticipates that the teenage years will be more challenging "because of how much society has changed and how difficult my own teenage years were." This can also be an opportunity to provide tweens or teenagers with preventive coaching or mental health support to break generational cycles. Jake, sober 12 years with four children under the age of nine, notes that he has been sure to get ahead of mental health issues with his children so that they may have a better chance of learning coping skills and avoiding self-medication at this stage. Cassie reveals that she is enjoying her son's independence; she says, "Social clicks are starting to form for him. That is hard for me and is bringing up some trauma, which I have been addressing with my therapist." Joan has enjoyed watching them reach milestones. She has found most recently that it has been hard to deal with the start of the pre-teen puberty and the emotional side of her oldest daughter because "I see a lot of me in her."

Early adolescence is when, besides experiencing hormonal changes, children begin to test limits with behaviors such as sexual experimentation, misuse of electronics, and substance use. Increasingly, youth seek independence from their parents, which often plays out in behaviors that seem detached, sullen, or dismissive.[22] Jennifer Senior describes, "Adolescence is especially rough on parents who don't have outside interests, whether it be work or a hobby, to absorb their interests as their child is pulling away. . . . It was as if the child, by leaving center stage, redirected the spotlight onto the parent's own life, exposing what was fulfilling about it and what was not."[23] Jennifer Barba adds, "PIR clients may encounter challenges related to setting boundaries, addressing potential substance use issues, experiencing dysregulated moods and setting limits around activities."

PIRs have specific stressors that differ from those of parents not in recovery, with fears around future substance use or dependence; 57.1 percent of parents surveyed who were not in recovery reported they do not fear that their children will develop an SUD. For the 42.9 percent who did, the main reasons, from greatest to least, were genetics, the child's personality type, general culture, and family culture. In contrast, a majority of the PIRs interviewed reported an intense fear about their tweens or teenagers starting to drink or use substances and developing an SUD in the future. On the other hand, 23.5 percent of the parents not in recovery reported, on a scale of 1 to 10 (low to high), a rating of 2 or 5 in level of severity of concern, with just 5.9 percent reporting a rating of 8.

PIRs expressed many more concerns about their teenagers starting use or developing substance use issues. Liz Modugno shares, "Often PIRs have experienced trauma and great consequences from their addictions. Trauma is often a contributor to addiction, but it is also a consequence of addiction. One symptom of trauma is hypervigilance, which is a consistent state of being alert and assessing for potential threats. If a person started drinking/using or has been negatively impacted during their tweens and teens by their addiction and now they are a parent to tweens and teens, they can be more hypervigilant of their child's behaviors." Sharon, sober for 24 years with adult children, identifies that her greatest worry has been "about my children inheriting this awful disease; both have a 50/50 chance due to their lineage." She has also found her greatest blessing has been watching them both flourish.

For PIRs of younger children, it was a matter of speculation regarding which parenting stage they anticipated would be the most challenging. Natasha predicts that the hardest parenting stage for her "will be when he is a teenager because of hormones and fear that he will become an addict, too." Chris admits, "I am terrified of having two teenage girls." Cassie anticipates that she will enjoy this stage the most because "He can watch himself and I can have my own life" but adds, "I think it will be challenging, letting go and praying he will be ok. I hope he does not have some of the issues my husband and I have had." Tracie worries more about her teens using substances as self-medication for anxiety or depression and if they began using alcohol or drugs before age 17. Violet admits, "I worry about it and have educated my son on his genetic inheritance (both parents). He understands the mental development and how critical it is for him not to drink in adolescent years to avoid becoming 'pickled.'" Nancy validates fears around substance use, revealing, "The most challenging stage was when our children were teenagers. Those times were filled with a ton of emotional ups and downs for the kids that we had a hard time understanding: drug use, strong pulling back and disappearing from us as parents and from the family unit. No longer sharing with us about their lives and feelings, hopes and dreams."

Despite research and interview responses, some PIRs have found this and the young adult stages to be the best fit for them. Marilyn, sober 22 years with adult children, reports, "The most joyful time is now. My children are adults, and watching them grow, mature and live successful lives while remaining close to me brings great satisfaction." Tracie asserts, "I love communicating with teens and being a part of their lives as they navigate social situations and school pressures. It's fun to spend time together (especially now that I am sober), and I feel like we enjoy many of the same things, so time together is beneficial for both, unlike when they were little, and there's very little 'reward' as a parent." Mason states, "Connecting with my 15-year-old son and 12-year-old daughter has been an amazing experience. Beyond the adorable ages and precious innocence, understanding and fathering a mature child has been very rewarding. Seeing them thrive mentally and socially warms my heart." Stacie agrees, "I love parenting my teenager, I love the person he has become, and I love hearing his take on things. Also, parenting him is not physically demanding. I am sad he's getting older and wish he wanted to spend more time with us, but I'm working on acceptance with that." At the same time, she also worries about his trying alcohol and drugs and what that may entail.

Some PIRs have shifted their perspectives. Cathy, sober for 23 years with a teenage son, shares, "During a custody battle, I worried constantly that he would end up suffering from depression, which might lead to addiction. I don't worry now. I don't see the same markers I saw in myself that might lead to addiction. He has better coping skills than I did. He is able to talk about his feelings and doesn't use food or romantic relationships or video games to regulate when he's upset. He apologizes easily, has empathy and insight and self-awareness and just seems so solid." She also is reassured that he would come to her to get help for substance use or mental health issues. Stacey has been able to reframe her fears, expressing, "I go back and forth worrying about losing a child to this disease and then thinking about how grateful I am to be an alcoholic because I love my life now. And if that is their path, hopefully, they would find recovery too and have a 'life beyond their wildest dreams.'"

Self-Disclosure to Children

The age at which PIRs tell their children *why* they are sober and about their SUDs differs. Some feel that information would overwhelm young children, while others believe normalizing the topic is beneficial. Cindy House, author of the recovery-based memoir *Mother Noise*, captures the internal conflict many PIRs have surrounding self-disclosure with their children. She describes this confusion with her son when he was ten years old, writing, "If I don't tell him soon, it could become a lie by omission, a distance between us, a secret that might leave him feeling like he doesn't really know me." She goes on to express her fear that "What if the information about my past works not as a warning but instead as a blueprint?"[24] Eventually, she becomes certain that "the telling" was the right choice for her and her son. Cindy states that many PIRs have approached or contacted her about "The need to talk to their kids about this and how my book made them step up their plans to do this. And I've talked to parents who already talked with their kids and the various outcomes of that were all good." There is not one correct way to handle self-disclosure; instead, it can be helpful to learn about how various PIRs have navigated this issue:

- "My girls knew I was in recovery right away, and they were 11 and 13 when I got sober. I believe it would be unfair not to include them in my recovery since they were unfortunate witnesses to my alcoholism. They were old enough to understand that I needed help and it was a great sense of peace for them knowing I had a recovery community. It made us closer and took any pressure off them to help me stay sober." —Tracie
- "I told my son when he was almost ten because he was asking more questions about the world, and I realized that his father or stepmother could tell him, and then he might feel like I'd lied to him, and I was afraid it would hurt our relationship. He's responded well, I think. It's an ongoing conversation. He asks me a lot of questions about substances and mental health." —Cathy
- "I would use discernment with the ages about alcohol and drugs as you would about sex. I think it's important to understand their mental development and go from there. I would also seek guidance from a professional." —Violet
- "We are going to talk about it at ten years old. We have mentioned what alcohol is and that we don't drink it." —Chris
- "Since day one, he has been going to meetings with me (son is now 12)." —Gina
- "At ages seven and 11, they know that I don't drink but that is it. I'm thinking before high school." —Joan
- "I was in recovery for nine years before my oldest was born. My recovery and fellowship has always been part of their lives." —Laura
- "The conversation came naturally over time. While discussing life, my kids would ask questions, and I would spoon-feed them what I thought was appropriate given their age and context of the conversation. One day, my teenage son asked me what drugs I had done . . . I told him 95% of the truth. It was humbling but created such

an amazing bond between us. I have no regrets about it. I believe my son respects me for who I am and is very proud to have me as a father." —Mason

- "We have always been open about our recovery, and the kids have asked us different kinds of questions depending on their developmental stage. We didn't wait for a certain age. Earlier in their lives, it just meant we were out at a 'meeting.' Later on, as they got older, they asked questions, or we brought up, how certain things connected to our recovery." —Nancy
- "My 15-year-old has known for a while. He was taken away from me when he was four and understood that Mom was sick and went away to get better. Then, I got him back when he was almost seven. At that point, we explained that I needed meetings to keep me healthy so that I didn't get sick again. Once he was about 11, I described to him in a general sense what addiction was and what it was like for me. At ages 12–14, I told him a lot about my active addiction. I want him to know what it looks like and that he is at a higher risk of having it since both of his biological parents have it. I want him to know what options he would have to treat it." —Stacie
- "My husband and I are both open and honest about our recovery. Both of my children have come to 12-step meetings since they were newborns. My daughter started asking questions about us not drinking and/or going to meetings around three years old. She responded with curiosity and continues to be very aware of alcohol in our presence because she knows it is outside of the norm as our house is alcohol-free. Now, at seven, she learns about alcohol in school and probably has much more knowledge about it than most children her age. I didn't necessarily choose when to tell them but instead made a choice that we wouldn't hide it from our children or make it seem like a forbidden topic." —Jackie

Parent Recovery Wisdom

PIRs and addiction treatment professionals highlight the following strategies and ideas for coping with the challenges of the various "dog years." They are categorized by: all stages; pregnancy and newborn; toddler and young child; tween, teenager, and young adult. Some are listed exactly as stated by the PIRs to capture their tone and message. The following suggestions are meant to provide options and are not intended to be used in their entirety.

All Stages

- Prioritize recovery and self-care because if your battery is drained, you will have nothing to give your child or family.
- Apply recovery principles to all areas of your life.
- Seek balance but recognize that it is not always possible.
- Allow your relationship with your children at each stage to be a gift of sobriety.
- Strive for patience, tolerance, and unconditional love for others and yourself.
- Know that you may need professional support at different stages.
- Recognize that past trauma may surface at different stages and address those symptoms promptly.
- Find child-friendly self-help meeting options.
- Bring your child with you for self-care or wellness-related activities if necessary.
- Find humor. 😊
- Connect with other PIRs!

Pregnancy and Newborn Stages

- Attend birthing and newborn parenting classes.
- Establish a support network when pregnant.
- Engage in healthy escapes.
- Create household routines.
- Ask for help! You cannot do it alone.
- Determine which partner is better at various aspects of care and delegate.
- It's okay not to know what you are doing.
- Remember that other parenting phases may be less intense.
- Do the best that you can do to integrate recovery and self-care into your day.
- Give yourself grace and know that you are doing the best you can at this time.

- Expect that you may not be operating or functioning as well as you did before having a newborn.
- Seek out new parent support groups and activities to decrease the sense of isolation.
- Acknowledge that each day is different and that this stage will get much easier with time.
- Remember that this is often a harder age for some and will transition to what could be a more joyful stage.

Toddler and Young Child Stages

- Explore passions beyond the family.
- Remember that children change and another stage may best suit you.
- Know that other parents also struggle with the younger years.
- Take "time outs."
- Get together with other parents to have adult time while all the children play.
- Determine age-appropriate boundaries.
- Lead by example in vulnerability and by seeking support as needed.
- Engage in healthy self-care activities with your child or begin to teach them different options.
- Figure out when you need downtime or more activity and adjust your schedule as possible.
- Open up age-appropriate lines of communication.
- Choose your battles.
- Find activities that you both enjoy doing.

Tween/Teenager/Young Adult Stages

- Foster a family culture of communication.
- Engage in preventive mental health and substance use care.
- Have children feel comfortable going to therapy and addressing issues ahead of time.
- Discuss the importance of your recovery.
- Encourage honesty before punishment.
- Expose tweens/teenagers to the positive culture of recovery and wellness.

- Allow tweens/teenagers to have their own cause-and-effect experiences.
- Detach with love.
- Protect your recovery.
- Be open about how their behaviors impact you and the family system.
- Talk about your feelings and create room for theirs.
- Be human and relatable.

Personal Journal Entries

July 16, 2011—17 weeks pregnant

I am trying to attend the women's recovery meeting, but I have honestly been too tired to go to meetings in the evenings and took a two-month break—the longest ever. I have been speaking with sober peers and helping others to keep connected. I can see how motherhood takes women away from self-help programs, and I have also heard of relapse stories.

Emotional sobriety is really important while pregnant. I could do more, but I am also working on putting less pressure on myself. This is a time to hunker down and be nurtured.

September 24, 2011—27 weeks pregnant

I feel somewhat disconnected, my mind cannot absorb the reality of being pregnant, of having a child. It is too huge to conceptualize, and words/thoughts almost cannot capture it.

I am thankful to have been practicing spiritual acts that have helped with my state of mind. I am able to identify the tricks my mind plays on me in the form of fearful thoughts. Pregnancy can challenge me in a way different than when I am preoccupied with myself. Someone else is involved, and their well-being is my focus.

March 8, 2012—Eve, three months old

I am slowly gaining confidence in myself in bringing Eve out in public (she is fine!). I worry and feel out of control, but I need to push myself so that we are mobile. She loves to be out and stimulated, and I am slowly learning how to coordinate things. I am not a nurturer by nature, but I will continue to work on this trait for Eve's sake.

March 21, 2014—Eve, two years old

I feel at capacity. I want to "veg out" and watch stupid TV. I have aspirations to write a book but lack dedication. I start and stop books, self-help meetings are an afterthought, and sleep is my #1 priority—goodnight!

9

Buzzkill

Sober Socializing in a Digital Age

"Boundaries are for you and me."

—Gina

SOCIALIZING IS A BASIC HUMAN NEED. Our biological history of communication and interaction is rooted in survival. Research suggests that our ancestors developed a basic form of language to share ideas and create tools to survive and evolve.[1] For a species to survive, members need to be able to band together to protect each other from predators. In our modern age, social interaction has mental health and health benefits beyond survival. Dr. Susan Pinker, a developmental psychologist and author of *The Village Effect*, describes, "Face-to-face contact releases a whole cascade of neurotransmitters and, like a vaccine, they protect you now, in the present, and well into the future. So simply shaking hands or giving someone a high-five is enough to release oxytocin, which increases your level of trust and lowers your cortisol levels, so it lowers your stress." She adds that social interactions generate dopamine, which gives a slight high and can naturally decrease pain.[2]

Socializing can protect against mental health and medical conditions. Meaningful friendships can bolster a strong sense of companionship, mitigate feelings of loneliness, improve life satisfaction, and increase self-esteem.[3] These positive effects are all protective factors for mental health issues. In a large meta-analysis, participants with stronger social relationships had a 50 percent higher chance of survival against well-established risk factors for mortality, such as physical inactivity and obesity.[4] Social isolation and loneliness can have a negative health impact, which has been equated with the effects of being obese, physically inactive, smoking 15 cigarettes daily; and is associated with a 50 percent increased risk of dementia.[5] Therefore, even those who tend to isolate socially should try to connect with others, however possible, for their wellness.

Parental Substance Use Culture

While socializing is proven healthy, the culture in many adult circles embraces unhealthy activities, such as alcohol and marijuana use. The past several decades have seen a notable shift toward drinking when preparing dinner, getting together with other parents, and attending children's birthday parties and other events. The frequency of substance use at other parents' houses and events varies nationwide. Many parents report that drinking and other substance use helps them manage stress—and, combined with social events, temporarily allows them to find escape and relief. Deidra Roach, medical project officer for the National Institute on Alcohol Abuse and Alcoholism, reported that "One reason that drinking is on the rise among women is that the norms around drinking have changed dramatically over the past 50 or so years. Up until the mid-20th century, it was considered socially unacceptable for women to drink in public, especially to the point of intoxication."[6] Trish Elizabeth, author and PIR, comments, "Aren't we also told that alcohol helps relieve stress in every commercial for the low-calorie seltzers marketed specifically for moms? Or the mugs that say to kids, 'Mommy drinks wine because of you'? Or a celebrity mom on Instagram justifying drinking alone in a closet because her kids were bugging her and being a mom is so hard? When did it become acceptable for mothers, whose job description is to take care of another human being who cannot take care of themselves, to drink a dangerous, mind-altering substance as their reward at the end of the day? Or as a commonly used method of handling the challenges of motherhood?"[7] Meanwhile, the norms for men have not undergone such a noticeable shift.

Understanding the parent substance use landscape involves knowing exactly how many parents are drinking alcohol or using marijuana—the two legal and most commonly abused substances. Between 2015 and 2019, 73.2 percent of children, *meaning more than 97 million children*, lived with a parent who drank alcohol, and 4.7 percent lived with a parent who had an alcohol use disorder; 12.2 percent of children, meaning more than 16 million children, had a parent who used marijuana, and 0.8 percent had a cannabis use disorder. Parents.com surveyed mothers to explore the drinking culture and more than 80 percent of the moms surveyed said the top reason they drink is to relax and unwind. Specifically, "some felt isolated and unfamiliar to themselves in new parenthood. Sitting back with a drink felt comforting, like a way to reclaim a part of their lives lost to parenthood."[8] Of the parents (both men and women) not in recovery who were surveyed for this book, 57 percent indicated that they decreased their drinking after becoming parents, 28.6 percent said their drinking remained the same, and 10.7 percent increased their use of alcohol.

Parents who drink excessively may find it comfortable to enter into an echo chamber of like-minded mothers and fathers in the school system, extracurricular activities, and the local community who use substances the same way they do. Coupled with social media posts, making light of substance use can add a layer of validation, minimization, and normalization. Liz Modugno, LICSW, LADC, validates that "One of the greatest social challenges I see is parents trying to find other sober or generally healthy parents with whom to spend time. Modern-day culture has emphasized drinking and drug use. PIRs often come into session and discuss how, 'at a play date I was offered a glass of wine,' 'during the football game, other parents are drinking during or after the game,' or 'a lot of the parents are vaping or smoking pot' while out in the community." Susan Berlin, LICSW, CASAC, ICADC, has many PIR clients who are professional men surrounded by happy hours, client dinners, and sports club events that revolve around drinking. Alcohol is used as a source of bonding and to ease social tensions.

PIRs from coast to coast have observed some extreme social scenes from a "sobering" perspective. Evelyn, sober for ten years, assesses her suburban community, stating, "It's been a while since I've socialized with people who drink or smoke pot, but that's in large part because the parents I know who aren't in recovery all drink and smoke and it's completely accepted—even when excessive." Tracie, sober for two years, notes, "Parents drink, drug and party a lot where I live. Alcohol and marijuana (edibles mostly) are a big part of the social scene in my town and were a part of most adults-only events and even ones where kids were present, including birthday parties, beach days, school events, holiday parties, neighborhood events, etc." Cassie, sober for 15 years, observes, "All of the parents at my son's school drink, and I am sure many use edible marijuana. There are cliques of kids based on the fact that their parents party together." Joan, sober for ten years has found alcohol and drinking to be "acceptable, provided and in some cases expected." Natasha, sober for six years observes that "everyone around my neighborhood drinks, but most of my friends are sober." Rebecca, sober for two years reflects, "Pot is legal here, so there's a pretty casual approach to using." Jackie, sober for 14 years explains that she and her husband were discussing the start of T-ball season again and "how parents will bring alcohol to drink in their tumblers to the practices or games. . . . I also vividly remember starting to go to birthday parties for children where the parents drank alcohol, which seemed bizarre to me at first, but I think it's quite common."

A few PIRs report living in areas with less of a substance use culture or have found a way to avoid it. Douglas, sober for 14 years, explains that he and his wife "surround ourselves with similar lifestyles, stay in the center, stick with moderate individuals and not around people who would have an issue with recovery." Stacie, sober for 11 years, has observed a shift in culture, stating there are "wine moms around me, but thankfully not drinking for health reasons has become trendy, so I feel less weird telling people I don't drink."

Sober Socializing

The social norm for parents of drinking alcohol and using marijuana can leave some PIRs feeling "different" than other parents, particularly those who are newly sober. These PIRs can also experience discomfort when socializing with extended family members who use substances. The boundaries that are necessary to set, particularly in early sobriety, can lead PIRs to feel like outsiders. Barba, LICSW, explains, "Social isolation is another significant challenge faced by PIRs. During recovery, individuals may need to distance themselves from old social circles that could trigger relapse or hinder their progress. This transition can leave them feeling disconnected and needing new, supportive relationships." PIRs must be honest with themselves, friends, and extended family about what they can expose themselves to. Evelyn recalls that it was hard for her to be around alcohol in early sobriety—whether with friends or for family occasions. She admits, "It just underscored feeling different and even 'less than' everyone else. So, I didn't go to many events I wanted to go to due to fear of relapse or of just being miserable." She has experienced a shift as she has entered longer-term recovery and "can go anywhere even if there is alcohol, and that doesn't bother me. It is still hard for me to get together in stressful situations where others are drinking to ease the tension, and I cannot." Tracie took a break from her social circle when she got sober and slowly gravitated back to select events. She shares, "I haven't had cravings, but I have found myself getting bored and wanting to go home once I have socialized for a few hours. It takes more mental effort to socialize sober, so I get tired quickly at larger events." She also emphasizes the importance of having other sober friends to normalize the experience. She adds, "When you go out for dinner with sober friends, ordering water, iced tea or soda doesn't feel weird." Taking breaks from intense holiday or regular events may be necessary temporarily or permanently—each PIR has a different tolerance for being around substance use. Claire, sober for six years, remembers saying to herself, "I don't ever want to drink again," but then realizing that "socially, it was a little uncomfortable without having my liquid buffer, but the benefits of *not* drinking outweighed that."

The parents not in recovery survey results demonstrate that PIRs may falsely assume that they are making all other parents feel awkward about their drinking. For example, 78.6 percent of parents not in recovery responded that they were comfortable drinking around sober parents. Of the 17.9 percent who were uncomfortable, the main reasons were feeling like they were "bothering or tempting them" and "feeling judged or badly about my usage."

While social environments vary, other PIRs have continued to either feel emotionally like an outsider or experience being excluded. Liz Modugno suggests listing the top five closest friends or loved ones in active addiction and then listing who the top five are in sobriety. If these PIRs have not developed close bonds yet, they should seek out more like-minded people in their inner circle through online and in-person self-help groups, spiritual groups, clubs, and so on. Joan acknowledges that "I *am* different—I don't drink" and explains that the most challenging aspect socially has been being excluded from alcohol-related social events. Mason, sober for 19 years, comments that he struggles "interacting with people once they morph into their 'buzzed' personality, and it can be annoying for me. It gets boring, and I check out mentally." Violet, sober for 18 years, still finds that she "wants to be a 'part of' when I am around people who drink, and I do feel like I did ruin my chance to have a glass of wine." She wants to do the "normal thing like the rest of the parents." Cassie lives in a heavy drinking area, and her family has been left out of social invitations because they are sober. She says, "Not that I want to hang out drinking, but my son gets upset because he is not invited." She also struggles with authentically connecting with the other mothers, describing, "The mothers bond over wine, so I don't have anything we can do together as our interests don't align."

In contrast, others have either found ease in socializing around substances or developed ways to navigate this landscape. Laura, sober for 38 years, has been everywhere with her family and explains, "My disease is in remission as long as I remember I have a disease." She has found that others don't usually notice she is not drinking. Marilyn, sober for 22 years, has felt different in a "good way," adding, "I don't find it hard not to drink around others, but I find myself not interested in socializing with those who need to drink to socialize." Natasha finds, "It's not hard for me. I am pretty open about my recovery, and I respect the choices of others." Sharon, sober for 24 years, finds that "having a solid recovery foundation has allowed me to go to events where alcohol is served without fear." She has also created a practice to "always let at least one person present know that I don't drink" to develop a sense of accountability. Jackie, sober for 14 years, explains, "The people I socialize with mostly know that I don't drink, so I haven't found it particularly challenging. I think that is because I built a strong foundation of friends in recovery when I first got sober, which normalized *not* drinking while socializing. To this day, I plan to either be with people I trust or have an exit plan for any event with alcohol because you never know how people will behave once they start drinking." Cathy, sober for 23 years, was addicted to opiates in her past and finds that "I don't ever miss drinking, and no one is doing drugs in my circles. I don't even notice when some parents are drinking at events."

While there are many strategies to manage socializing sober in environments with substance use, PIRs should also create opportunities to spend time at substance-free events and with others engaged in the same lifestyle. Rosemary O'Connor, in her book *A Sober Mom's Guide to Recovery*, shares that when she got sober, "I thought my life was over, that I had been sentenced to a life of lack and limitation. I feared that, without drinking, I would have no personality at all and would become like a hole in the donut—just a dull, boring woman."[9] She is not alone; many have these same apprehensions in early sobriety. Jackie notes, "If I didn't have role models in early recovery to show me that being sober is actually *more* fun than drinking, I think my life would be very different today." David, sober for 19 years, enjoys his sober lifestyle and peers, and this has allowed him to avoid socializing with the substance-using parent crowd. Rosemary O'Connor explains how she created a new culture and social life for herself in sobriety, "For about five years, a group of us 'sober sisters' spent most of our free time together. We threw some of the greatest parties, including luaus, pool parties, birthday, and sobriety parties. . . . We ran triathlons and marathons and played in sober softball leagues. . . . We got our kids together and had slumber parties and picnics at the beach. We laughed, shared meals, and drank *a lot* of coffee. Best of all, we modeled for our children that life can be a lot of fun without drugs and alcohol."[10]

Social Media and Electronics

Technology has simultaneously advanced and disconnected our society. Social media and electronic communication are interwoven into our culture. While this has many benefits in terms of efficiency and innovation, there are many downsides, including impacts on mental health, addiction, and isolation.

Dopamine Connection

Social media platforms have been designed to trigger the pleasure and reward centers in the brain—mimicking substance use. Anna Lembke, MD, is the medical director of Addiction Medicine at Stamford

University and author of the book *Dopamine Nation*. She draws parallels between the way that substance use and electronics stimulate the brain, explaining, "We're living in a time of unprecedented access to high-reward, high-dopamine stimuli: drugs, food, news, gambling, shopping, gaming, texting, sexting, TikToking, Instagramming, YouTubing, tweeting . . . the increased numbers, variety and potency are staggering. The smartphone is the modern-day hypodermic needle, delivering digital dopamine 24/7 for a wired generation."[11] As noted previously, humans are biologically primed for connection, and social media capitalizes on this need, increasing the potential for abuse and addiction.

Dopamine is a neurotransmitter in the brain that is involved in reward processing. The more dopamine a substance or behavior can release, or at greater speed in the brain's reward pathway, the more addictive that substance or behavior is. Substances do not need to contain actual dopamine, but they prompt its release into the reward pathway. This explains why so many different substances, foods, and behaviors can elicit these reward sensations—each leading to varying amounts of dopamine release. It is a normal response to want to reexperience something pleasurable, which leads to repeating behaviors such as eating, playing video games, checking social media, and using substances. To make matters worse, the brain neuroadapts, meaning it develops tolerance over time to this process, leading to an actual "dopamine deficit state." In this state of mind, normally pleasurable activities release less natural dopamine. The result can be an accelerated use or addiction to the high-dopamine substance(s) or behaviors and decreased engagement in the lower-dopamine "natural high" activities.[12]

Impact on PIRs

Given that substance use has a high-dopamine reward, it makes sense that individuals with SUDs or those in recovery may have an increased vulnerability to electronic-based addictive behaviors. Edward Tufte, a statistician, bridges the gap between electronics and addiction, stating, "There are only two industries that call their customers 'users': illegal drugs and software."[13] Research indicates that drug use may predict a high risk for internet addiction and that individuals with an internet addiction have an increased chance of developing an SUD.[14] Susan Berlin, LICSW, CASAC, ICADC has noticed that screen time tends to increase when a client stops substance use, seemingly as a way to self-soothe or continue to medicate the emotional states underneath, and that this can easily evolve into compulsive online behaviors. Liz Modugno has observed that "Social media also has its own addictive qualities. Several clients I work with in recovery struggle with addiction to their phones, social media, pornography and/or sports gambling. When people are engaging in these activities, they are mimicking substance use. Brain scans show similar patterns of brain activity from addiction to substances and addiction to electronics."

The movie *The Social Dilemma* integrates research and information from social media executives, developers, and engineers who reveal how these platforms manipulate people as "products" used to increase profits. Chamath Palihapitiya, former vice president of growth at Facebook, has said that these companies "want to psychologically figure out how to manipulate you as fast as possible and then give you back that dopamine hit."[15] Joan admits, "I am addicted to Facebook and Instagram but have a system for what I do and won't do in terms of not 'liking' people bragging and posting pictures about drinking." Natasha acknowledges that she needs to check the motives of her posts and attention-seeking behaviors, as well as how she internalizes other people's posts. Although unaware of dopamine-related research, she notices "addictive behaviors in myself with response to my phone and usage and also with the ritualistic ways in which I check things." Violet has a love/hate relationship with electronics and social media, finding that they can be extremely useful and informative, but then they can "lead me to check out of reality and become addictive at times." Jackie reported the same dynamic with her phone; while she has enjoyed connecting with people she has previously lost touch with, it can also be addictive and a "time filler." She is aware that her brain is wired toward addictive behaviors and sometimes deletes social media apps to have more control over her usage. Stacie has a positive and negative perspective. She believes she spends too much time on social media but she also uses it for her business. She enjoys connecting with others, but "I hate seeing news on social media, and I don't like seeing all the division and hatred toward people who think differently than me."

The powerful imagery and illusion of connectedness through social media can exacerbate a "fear of missing out"—the FOMO phenomenon. Dr. Lembke notes, "Social media has contributed to the problem of the false self by making it far easier for us, and even encouraging us, to curate narratives of our lives that are far from reality."[16] These platforms allow parents and other individuals to become their own public relations representatives and to post images that convey what they want others to see of their lives and what they may ideally wish their lives were. Part of this world involves posting pictures and videos that glorify social events, substance usage, and being "part of" social and online groups. A regressive element to these online ecosystems can lead individuals to recreate earlier life phases. PIRs in early sobriety may feel left out of social events that they either turned down or were not invited to. In the past, the event would occur, and the individual would not see it happening in real time. Now, they often see social media posts of others at these events, signaling being left out and providing a lens into their former lifestyle. While social media use has created more online interactions, it has decreased authenticity and quality of the connections. "We get rewarded in these short-term signals—hearts, likes, thumbs up—and we conflate that with value and truth," adds Tristen Harris, co-founder of the Center for Humane Technology and former design ethicist at Google.[17] Much like the hangover from using substances, the temporary feeling of approval can leave individuals with a void more significant than before they posted, along with the urge to get that feeling back. He adds that while we have evolved to care what people in our social circle think of us, "Were we evolved to be aware of what 10,000 people think of us? We were not evolved to have social approval being dosed to us every five minutes."[18] Jennifer Barba finds that "social media can contribute to feelings of inadequacy and comparison, potentially leading to self-esteem issues. PIRs may compare their recovery progress to that of others, which can foster self-doubt or discouragement. Moreover, excessive reliance on electronics and social media can contribute to feelings of isolation and disconnection from real-life relationships." Melany Montrond, LCSW and director of clinical operations at Lynch Wellness Professional Group, has seen that "Social media has impacted PIRs in various ways—what they observe in others living their 'old life' and then tend to deeply reflect if it is necessary to end relationships as they could lead to regression. There are times when social media platforms can be powerful, thus making viewers believe that addiction to drinking, shopping and gambling are supposed to be a normal part of everyday life. They do a great job of selfishly targeting consumers without regard for the harm being caused." Mason, father of six-, 12-, and 15-year-old children, "tried social media for one year and learned that it is very empty and a waste of time. My life is far richer without it and not worth sacrificing precious time with my children in order to read about a stranger's life."

While a large body of research and anecdotal evidence focuses on the harms and negative aspects of social media, there are also positive impacts and benefits. Evelyn described how "I was a recovery advocate and used social media to reach others who were struggling or in recovery and looking for a community. So, in that sense, social media brought a lot of positivity into my life personally and professionally, as it relates to recovery." However, now that she is not engaged in that work, she filters what she views to avoid those FOMO feelings. Cathy explains, "A few years ago, I saw another parent announce her three years in recovery, and it inspired me to stop hiding it." Chase, sober for 17 years, shares, "I had connected with a deceased friend's wife on Facebook. Her late husband was my best friend growing up, and he passed away in his 20s, leaving behind a 6-month-old son. She asked me to meet her and her son, who was now ten years old, and to tell him stories of his dad and me from when we were younger so he could get an idea of what his dad was like. It was one of the most rewarding blessings of my life." Sharon shares that she "uses social media as a platform for empowerment." Jennifer Barba has found some positive recovery advantages in that these platforms "offer easier access to recovery resources, support groups, and educational materials. PIRs can benefit from online platforms that provide virtual meetings, online communities, and a wealth of information to enhance their recovery journey. Social media platforms and online recovery communities also enable PIRs to connect with others who share similar experiences, fostering a sense of belonging, encouragement and a space to share struggles and achievements."

Impact on Children

A majority of children and teenagers use social media and electronics. According to the surgeon general's 2023 advisory *Social Media and Youth Mental Health*, up to 95 percent of youth ages 13–17 report using a social media platform, with more than a third saying that they use it "almost constantly." While age 13 is the most common age minimum for social media platforms, 40 percent of eight- to 12-year-olds use them.

Many PIRs expressed concern regarding the genetic component of SUDs and how that could impact their children. A similar level of awareness was present surrounding the impact of electronic and social media usage in potentially increasing this predisposition. Thomas Joiner, PhD, a professor at Florida State University, was co-author of a research study that found a causal connection between screen time, suicide rates, and mental health in youth. He encourages parents to track their children's screen time, reporting, "There is a concerning relationship between excessive screen time and risk for death by suicide, depression, suicidal ideation and suicidal attempts. All those mental health issues are very serious. I think it's something parents should ponder."[19] His study considered the alarming trend reported by the CDC of depression and suicide rates for teens between the ages of 13 and 18, which have increased 31 percent since 2010. In addition, a national survey showed that the number of adolescents reporting symptoms of severe depression rose 33 percent. These increases were largely in teenage girls, whose suicide rate soared by 65 percent, with the rate of those suffering from severe depression increasing by 58 percent.[20] The study found that the rise in mental health problems among teens since 2010 coincides with increased accessibility of cell phones. In 2012, about one-half of Americans owned smartphones; by 2015, 92 percent of teens and young adults had one, and their screen time also rose. Researchers discovered that 48 percent of teenagers who spent five or more hours per day on electronic devices reported suicide-related behavior compared with 28 percent of adolescents who spent less than an hour using electronic devices.[21] Additionally, the surgeon general's advisory said adolescents who spent more than three hours per day on social media faced double the risk of experiencing poor mental health outcomes, including symptoms of depression and anxiety.[22]

Many PIRs are keenly aware that their children have an increased predisposition for developing an SUD and that social media has an additional dopamine-priming effect. When they noticed their children's overuse, many created clear parameters. The few PIRs less aware of the research and connection were open to learning more. Evelyn, the mother of a 20-year-old daughter and 17-year-old son, has observed that her son grew up with social media his entire life, and "I can see what it's done to his attention span, which is almost nonexistent." Cassie has a nine-year-old son and has thought ahead, stating, "I do set restrictions so that he cannot get on sites that are not age-appropriate. This winter, he is playing hockey, soccer and basketball and is involved with Cub Scouts. We also started seasonal camping to keep him outside, active and off of electronics." Cathy has a 15-year-old son and says, "When he was younger, we had a lot of conversations about screens, and I talked a lot about how people sometimes use things to numb out or feel better or soothe, and that it was worrisome. I never had to set clear rules for him because he has always been able to use screens in moderation. This is one thing that makes me worry less about addiction being a possibility for him." While Joan, mother of seven- and 11-year-old daughters, admits to her overuse of social media, she has not changed her personal use but is concerned for her children and limits their time and access to social media. Stacie, mother of six-, seven-, and 15-year-old children, explains, "I believe it releases dopamine and can be very addictive. Setting times for no phones has helped me realize how much of a habit picking up my phone is." Violet, a mother to six-, 12-, and 15-year-old children, shares her awareness and has linked her children's devices to hers for monitoring. She uses her ability to turn their access on and off as leverage for them to complete homework and chores, validating, "I think teaching kids how to manage their time and schedule and educating them on addictive pathways will be an ongoing discussion."

Many PIRs have learned to manage uncomfortable feelings and moods through healthy coping skills and self-care. This allows them to be more attuned to their overuse of electronics to avoid discomfort and boredom. Tristen Harris elaborates, "When we are lonely, uncomfortable or afraid then we have a digital pacifier for ourselves, atrophying our own ability to deal with that."[23] Jackie endorses that she is aware of the research and "I see technology teaching children that they can have immediate gratification when bored at any time when we should be teaching children to tolerate those feelings because that's what they will experience in life." She adds that she has prioritized socialization by not allowing devices at meals and not using them as a "babysitter." She has found video calls a helpful way for her children to stay in touch with family members at appropriate times.

Jaron Lanier, one of the founders of virtual reality and author of *Ten Arguments for Deleting Your Social Media Accounts Right Now*, believes that part of the danger of social media is not apparent harm or exploitation but "the gradual, slight, imperceptible change in your behavior and perception that is the product."[24] Susan Berlin has observed FOMO with more young adult clients for instance when they decline a party and then see images of their friends at these events on social media. Susan emphasizes the importance of having a sober community of friends where one can find an authentic sense of self and belonging, critical to long-term recovery and in filling the gaps of those places that they don't belong in the same way that they used to. Similarly, Jill Griffin, LICSW, LADC, has observed that parents often post everything their child does on social media, thus giving the message that what they do needs approval and validation from others. These shifts in emotions and behaviors are subtle and occur over time—which is the intention of these platforms.

The good news? Making changes in social media use results in dramatic shifts in the overall well-being of children and teenagers. Research on college-aged youth found that limiting social media use to 30 minutes daily over three weeks significantly decreased the severity of depression. Additional research in youth found that deactivation of a social media platform for four weeks improved life satisfaction, depression, and anxiety by about 25–40 percent, similar to the effect of various forms of therapy.[25]

Parent Recovery Wisdom

The following strategies are from PIRs, addiction treatment, and technology professionals for managing sober socializing, social media, and electronics. Some are listed exactly as stated to capture their exact tone and message. The following suggestions are meant to provide options and are not intended to be used in their entirety.

Social Events

The following are strategies for navigating social events and dynamics with friends, acquaintances, coworkers, or other parents who drink and/or use substances.

Friend and Coworker Events

- Accept invitations to events through a lens of recovery—check in with how you are feeling and remain flexible to cancel plans if you do not feel strong that day.
- Say "maybe" to an event to give yourself time to consider what you really want to do.
- Decline invitations.
- Expand your social circle to include people living a healthy and/or recovery lifestyle to increase socializing opportunities.
- Decide how you will respond to questions about not using substances or practice refusal skills (e.g., "I am sober," "I am on medication," "I stopped drinking and smoking pot because it was not working well for me anymore").
- Remember that your sobriety is more important than any social event.
- Take a break from socializing with friends who do not support or understand your sobriety.
- Be clear about how long you plan to stay at an event if it would help to manage others' expectations.
- Remember that many people focus more on what they drink or use and less on what you do.
- Host an event that is comfortable socially for you.
- Spend time with friends during the day or participate in activities that do not include substances.
- Avoid "people pleasing" because this involves trying to keep others happy while neglecting your own needs.
- BYOD: Bring Your Own Drinks (e.g., seltzer, soda, iced tea, etc.).
- Examine your intention for attending the social event (living vicariously through others versus celebrating a loved one).

Extended Family Events

The following are strategies for navigating social events and dynamics with extended family members who drink and/or use substances.

- Set limits around time spent in stressful family situations.
- Have a non-alcoholic drink in your hand to decrease the likelihood of questions.

- Create a code word with a loved one or friend for check-ins or to leave the event early.
- Reach out for support in setting boundaries with family members.
- Ask your family to have non-alcoholic beverages on hand.
- Decide how you will respond to questions about not drinking, considering that family members may have prior knowledge about your sobriety.
- Ensure you can leave a difficult event when you want to by having or arranging for your own transportation.
- Recognize that family events may elicit more emotions and stress than other settings.
- Make an effort to spend time with family members one-on-one or in a smaller group if the large events are too stressful.
- Bring a friend or other loved one to a family function for additional support.
- Attend therapy and/or coaching before the event to increase resilience.
- Attend self-help groups for coping with other family members who may have SUDs (e.g., Al-Anon, ACOA, Nar-Anon, Learn 2 Cope, C.A.R.E.S.).
- Arrange for a sober peer to be available for you to call or text during the event.
- Spend the most time at the event with a family member(s) with whom you have the healthiest relationship.

Social Media and Electronics Solutions:

The following strategies are for finding balance and boundaries with social media and establishing a healthy relationship with electronics.

For Self

- Utilize the "Screen Time" feature on your iPhone to monitor your time on various apps.
- Delay social media until later in the day to prevent an early dopamine hit.
- Limit phone notifications.

- Set the tone for the day by starting the morning with a healthy and electronic-free activity.
- Delete apps that pull your attention and have a negative impact.
- Check in with yourself before and after engaging in activities on your phone to feel the impact on your nervous system and adjust use accordingly.
- Take an electronic or "high-dopamine" activity cleanse to recalibrate balance and increase pleasure in simple activities.
- Leave your phone in another room for periods.
- Set a timer or a precise time period for use instead of during spare time throughout the day.
- Add recovery or wellness-focused apps as an alternative to apps with negative content.
- Check in about "balance" in your relationship with electronic devices.
- Designate screen-free time daily and/or a regular "digital detox."

For Parenting

- Talk with other parents about creating shared norms in the school or community.
- Consider what your family "feeds" their brains with electronics.
- Educate your children about the benefits and dangers of social media (see the surgeon general's 2023 advisory on *Social Media and Youth Mental Health*).
- "Friend," follow, or otherwise connect with your children on social media to view their activity.
- Define times for use, such as after responsibilities are completed.
- Instill that electronics are a reward and not a privilege.
- Utilize the iPhone "Family Sharing" feature to monitor your children's app usage and set time limits.
- Place more habit-forming apps onto the iPhone "Screen Time" limits feature that would require parental approval for any or extended use.
- Role model mindfulness and moderation around your electronic usage.

- Ensure that social media is not used within one hour of bedtime and does not interfere with adolescents' minimum requirement of eight hours of sleep per night.
- Teach your children age-appropriate digital literacy (e.g., texting etiquette, understanding that digital footprints are permanent, guidelines for engaging with strangers, etc.).
- Encourage healthy online social support and phone, text, and video calls with friends.
- Keep in mind that research has shown that a *combination of* social media limits and boundaries, along with adult–child discussion around social media use, leads to the best outcomes for youth.[26]
- Watch the movie *The Social Dilemma* together with children over the age of 11 or 12 and discuss.
- Create a family media plan (healthychildren.org).
- Designate mealtimes and other family activities as electronic-free times.
- Provide your children with alternative activities or interactions.
- Do not have any devices in the bedroom before or during sleep.
- Delay the onset of social media use as long as possible (recommendation is not until high school).
- Explore smartphone alternatives for tweens and teens (e.g., Pinwheel, flip phones, "dumbphones," social media–free phones).

Social Media Screening

The American Psychological Association suggests periodic screening of social media by adolescents; this can allow you and your child(ren) to be aware of the following indicators of problematic use and to receive additional support if needed:

1. Do you tend to use social media even when you want to stop or realize it is interfering with necessary tasks? Yes/No
2. Do you spend an excessive amount of effort to ensure continued access to social media? Yes/No
3. Do you have an intense craving to use social media? Yes/No
4. Are you repeatedly spending more time on social media than intended? Yes/No

5. Are you lying or engaging in deceptive behavior to retain access to social media use? Yes/No
6. Have you had a loss or disruption of significant relationships or educational opportunities because of media use? Yes/No[27]

Personal Journal Entries

May 8, 2023—Eve, 11 years old

I am reflecting on my perception of socializing with other parents. At points, I had felt differently about hanging out with parents who drink and found it less appealing. Josh pointed out that we are different and that I should accept that. I guess I felt that because I am alright with others drinking (within reason), they would want to be or feel comfortable around us.

I appreciate that we can go to social events with other parents and that a majority can drink, hold conversations, and not turn into other people. I can't identify with that because that's not how I would have drunk.

Having our daughter tell us how grateful she is that we don't drink was so reinforcing. We made this life choice so many years ago, and the gifts continue.

May 20, 2023

I feel like I am feeding my daughter poison when I let her on the iPad for too long or for activities that seem overstimulating. I can see the addictive nature of electronics, and knowing her genetics, it leads me to want to be cautious for her.

I have seen her melt down after too much use, and it mimics actual substance withdrawal . . . scary to watch. Their minds are so pure, and it is our obligation to protect them from things that may seem benign.

June 25, 2023, 10:03 p.m. Sunday: Journal Entry from Eve—age 11

"I never thought I would ever feel this way about a video game, but I have thought about this for a while and I think I'm gonna take a break from my iPad. No matter how much I want it, I just can't get as addicted as I did this weekend. I want normal life back, living in nature, friends, family, working on the house, spending time with each other, animals, quad, movies, TV, school, pets, sports, music, Montana, Martha's Vineyard, being in the moment. Every time I think about my friends on their phones all the time, I just wish we could go back in time and just enjoy life itself, no electronics! I've come to realize family and life first and nonsense next to never. I LOVE you life, the way you are! Thank you. I'm SO thankful to be here. I love everyone in my life! ♡ Eve"

10

Recovery Pride

"Addiction is a disease that doesn't discriminate. It's actually an issue that has a solution. Recovery is real. And when we stand up and speak out, we put a face on the solution, and we help other people who don't know the faces or the solution. That's what the movement should be—standing up and speaking out. And it is happening."[1]

—William Moyers

Shame

THE TERM "SHAME" carries a heavy and dark weight. The definition can be even more ominous: "A painful emotion caused by consciousness of guilt, shortcoming, or impropriety" and "a condition of humiliating disgrace or disrepute."[2] According to Dr. Brené Brown, who researches shame and is a PIR herself, the power of shame is so great that it actually "derives its power from being unspeakable . . . shame hates having words wrapped around it. If we speak shame, it begins to wither."[3] In contrast, guilt is an adaptive emotion that can make individuals feel bad about specific actions while maintaining a positive sense of self. Shame is a maladaptive emotion and makes individuals feel bad about themselves.[4] Individuals in recovery often feel able to connect better to therapists or recovery coaches with lived experience or who engage in advocacy for those with SUDs. Jennifer Barba, LICSW, has found meaning in supporting her clients' shift in their relationship with recovery. She states, "In some ways, it has been easy when clients know that I own recovery homes in the area. They understand my passion for providing a safe and supportive environment to those in recovery. This decreases the stigma one may feel with a therapist."

The topic of SUDs and having this diagnosis elicits shame—tragically leading individuals to compartmentalize, escalate use, avoid help, refuse identification, lack vulnerability, feel judged, and remain dangerously silent. The shame of having an SUD can feed into the cycle of addiction and treatment avoidance. However, shame is not unique to those with SUDs. Everyone has experienced it; many fear talking about it, and the less it is talked about, the more control it has. Addiction has multiple implicit levels of shame. A primary level forms from the negative behaviors engaged in during active use. The secondary level is the admission of having an SUD diagnosis and wrestling with self-image. Additional layers can be self-imposed, lie within a family system, or be derived socially and culturally. This often includes the view that addiction is a moral failing or a lack of willpower. Shame is so powerful that research indicates it can elevate the risk of developing addiction. Specifically, in individuals with notable depression levels and endorsed levels of shame, alcohol and gambling problems could be predicted. Shame mediated the connection between depression and these addictive behaviors—priming the depressive pathways.

In contrast, those more prone to *guilt* were less likely to engage in alcohol use.[5] Cindy House, author of *Mother Noise*, writes about the insidious nature of shame as a PIR. "When my husband and I moved to New Haven, I stayed quiet about my past, because I felt certain none of the other moms or dads were hiding a background like mine. Then, one day I saw a Facebook post from Sherry, the mother of one of my son's friends. She wrote, 'Sometimes the thing holding you back is the belief that something is holding you back. Blessed to be in recovery today' . . . I've been watching how the other parents treat Sherry, to see whether they accept her into the community. I'm not proud of this. Even now, more than twenty years after getting clean, I assume people would reject me if they knew—and, more importantly, they would reject my son."[6] Natasha, sober for six years, believes that individuals in recovery sometimes feed into the issue because they "talk about addiction in a shameful way."

PIRs have differing feelings about the shame and even guilt surrounding their addiction. Some felt it more in early sobriety and have slowly transitioned to a place of gratitude and pride; for others, it still surfaces in certain situations. Will, sober for 16 years, felt shame in early sobriety and did not like talking about it. He has transitioned to feeling, "It's my most valuable possession. Nothing comes above recovery." Sharon, sober for 24 years, felt "Guilt and shame all of the time, but less so the longer I stay sober. One of the reasons I encourage people to engage in therapy is to unpack some of the deeply rooted false narratives." Steve, sober for 16 years, also felt shame early on, which has transitioned to immense pride. Rebecca, sober for two years, states, "I'm 99% pride and 1% shame. I'm committed to countering shame and talking openly with other mothers in recovery about forgiving themselves for their drinking and focusing on what actions they can take today to recover and heal from their mistakes." Mason admits that after being sober for 19 years, "I have experienced both at length. Feeling superior and judgmental toward others and also feeling like an outcast at times." Joan, sober for ten years, has also experienced a shift and explains, "I didn't talk about it in the beginning. I was worried about how people would respond. Would they like me? Would I be invited to places? Now I'm very proud to share that I have been sober for almost ten years and don't care what people think." Chase, sober for 17 years, discloses past guilt and shame because he was not the father he wanted to be when in active addiction. However, getting sober before his youngest daughter was born has given him "a chance to do things differently from the start." He shifted his experience to "mostly pride—I believe I'm a miracle and should have been a statistic." Cassie, sober for 15 years, feels generally proud of all she has accomplished in sobriety but struggles explicitly when she is not invited to events because she does not drink. Sober for two years, Tracie expresses that she has felt both emotions, stating, "The shame I felt as an active alcoholic was the worst feeling in the world—especially because I was also a parent. The shame is getting less and less, and I have forgiven myself for my past behavior. I feel extreme pride in being sober because it's the toughest thing I have ever done." Dr. Brené Brown describes how the shame process can dissipate over time, "If we can share our story with someone who responds with empathy and understanding, shame can't survive. Self-compassion is also critically important, but because shame is a social concept—it happens between people—it also heals best between people. A social wound needs a social balm, and empathy is that balm."[7]

Some PIRs have more consistent positive feelings—recovery alleviates their shame. Donna Aligato, a recovery advocate, notes, "Addiction may be the last of our hidden diseases, and recovery, the world's best-kept secret."[8] Natasha states, "I do not feel any shame at all. I am comfortable with the fact that I am an addict and know that I am made this way and have no control over my disease." Marilyn, sober for 22 years, expresses that "I feel a sense of pride knowing that I have maintained long-term sobriety." Jackie notes, "I have never felt ashamed as a parent in recovery or of my past because, by the time I became a parent, I was six years sober and had done the work on myself to shed the shame of addiction." David, who has been sober for 19 years, adds, "I can't help it; I'm proud. I view it as a strength and am never feeling shame." Chris, sober for 16 years, proudly states, "It is the single greatest thing I have done in my life. I guarantee I would not have the quality of life I have today if I wasn't a PIR." Alex, sober for 12 years, has not experienced any shame since he has remained sober—as opposed to the demoralization he had felt during relapses. Evelyn, sober for ten years, notes, "For all of the shame I felt about my addiction when I was active, I feel even more pride being in recovery."

Other PIRs vacillate between pride and shame depending on their emotions and external situations. Violet, sober for 18 years, tends to experience shame around individuals she doesn't know well and who do not have the same lived experience and trials that she has overcome. Stacie, sober for 11 years, generally feels pride in her recovery. She reveals that uncomfortable feelings "creep in when my younger two children do something for the first time and I miss it" because it reminds her of all she had not seen after she temporarily lost custody of her son due to her past addiction. Douglas, sober for 14 years, also experiences an ebb and flow to these feelings, stating, "Always grateful, and that is 'a spoonful of medicine.' There have been times when I struggle with pride. I wish that I got sober younger, knowing it would have been better if I never was an addict." Dan Lynch, LADC-1, CIP finds when working with PIRs that "discussing topics about the success of their children being raised with a sober lifestyle and what it means for them to be a good parent gives them a sense of pride."

Not all shame is bad; the antidote to shame and secrecy is sunlight and honesty. Destructive shame feeds the cycle of negative emotions and behaviors. In contrast, prosocial shame is predicated on the idea that shame can be useful and provide containment within society. The prosocial shame cycle involves an individual engaging in a maladaptive behavior, embracing radical honesty without being shunned, which leads to acceptance and healing. Prosocial shame can create a healthy family culture. Parents often believe hiding their mistakes and imperfections and highlighting their best selves is ideal for their children. This, in turn, can have the opposite effect by leading children to feel that love is conditional. Ironically, parents opening up about their difficulties and hard days can create emotional space for their children to share about their own.[9] This requires a willingness by parents to be humble and vulnerable—traits fostered in the recovery process.

Understanding the truth about addiction and how it compares to other medical or psychological conditions is important to treatment and advocacy. Susan Berlin, LICSW, CASAC, ICADC, emphasizes that,

> I am very clear that addiction is NOT a moral issue, that none of us woke and said "I want to be an addict, I want to drive drunk, I want to miss my kid's school activities because I was too high to drive" . . . Addiction is a symptom of something greater and getting help for this disease (and I speak of it as a disease) is not different from getting help for your thyroid or kidneys or hot flashes. Addiction is a medical issue, but by the time we seek help, it is often out of control or headed there. Reducing shame, normalizing the struggle and "comparing in" with others as opposed to "comparing out" is also helpful.

Liz Modugno, LICSW, LADC, is encouraged about the societal shift, noting, "Witnessing several parents become sober is an amazing and life-changing decision. It is one of the most difficult things someone can do, yet there is a stigma around saying you are sober. . . . There has been a great shift, especially among groups of sober parents. There is a pride in overcoming addiction and creating a new, healthy, sober lifestyle."

Anonymity and Public Self-Disclosure

Many individuals in recovery from SUDs keep their addiction a secret from loved ones, acquaintances, and colleagues. The foundation of most 12-step programs is anonymity, and this allows newcomers to feel safe to join and existing group members to continue attending, knowing their identity will be protected. While there are many other self-help group options, anonymity is often a cornerstone. Anonymity saves lives. However, while the principle of anonymity is crucial to the world of recovery, it also implies that having an SUD or even getting sober from one should be hidden. 12-step programs such as Alcoholics Anonymous were created with the tradition of anonymity, which proves that historically, alcoholism has held a stigma, and the principle of anonymity was intended to shield members from this. Alcoholics Anonymous Tradition 11 states, "Our public relations policy is based on attraction rather than promotion; we need always to maintain personal anonymity at the level of press, radio and films."[10] This refers to publicly disclosing *membership* in one of these 12-step programs and not the individual's choice to reveal personally or publicly that they are "sober" or "in recovery" from an SUD.

The documentary *The Anonymous People*, directed by Greg Williams, addresses the idea that the 12-step culture embraces anonymity for many beneficial reasons. However, over time, those in long-term recovery may become paranoid about ever revealing to others that they are sober. In other words, the secrecy that is protective in early sobriety may eventually feed the stigma later on around having an SUD. It also may prevent sober individuals from helping others in the community or their family because no one knows that they are in recovery. "Anonymity is not secrecy"[11] is an essential concept—PIRs who never share that they are practicing a recovery lifestyle can increase their own shame and prevent others from seeing that there is hope. The movie discusses a movement of individuals identifying personally or publicly as "a person in long-term recovery." This positioning also emphasizes the solution for addiction and focuses less on the problem and past destruction. More than 23 million adults, or 10 percent of Americans, identify as being in recovery from a past SUD, with parents and non-parents being just as likely to be in recovery.[12] William White, a researcher on addiction and its history, believes that how the media covers celebrity addiction and recovery has impacted societal stigma, explaining, "The issue of addiction is incredibly visible within the culture. And we have people heading to rehab one more time following their latest crash-and-burn experience, also very visible. But then, the irony is, the second people achieve stability, they virtually disappear from the airwaves."[13] He firmly believes that the lack of dialogue around recovery is a missing component of SUD awareness and treatment nationwide. "So, the recovery story has yet to be told. And what the advocacy movement is doing is challenging a vanguard of people in all walks of life, including people who are in a very visible position, whose story would be very powerful in changing attitudes and beliefs in this country, to tell their recovery story and *not* to just retell their addiction story."[14] Chris Herren, former NBA player, founder of the Herren Foundation for recovery advocacy and featured athlete in the ESPN recovery documentary *Unguarded*, shares that he hopes the impact of speaking publicly to youth will lead them to say, "It's kind of cool to be sober. Like, recovery's cool, you know? It's not a sign of weakness. It's not a sign of regret and shame. It's not a scarlet letter. It's not any of that." As a PIR, Herron gives his recovery anniversary chips to his children and reveals, "They know when it's coming, and they look forward to it, and they keep them on their dresser. The little trophies we share together. I'm a sober dad . . . There's nothing better than that."[15]

PIRs in various forms of media and publications have a unique opportunity to touch the lives of others with their stories while also opening themselves to judgment. Connecting a real face to a story is necessary for replacing negative judgments with compassion and understanding. The courage of PIRs to make their voices heard and to normalize the recovery process has contributed to this movement. Storytelling itself is part of the self-help culture and has many healing qualities. Brenda Wilhelmson, author of *Diary of an Alcoholic Housewife*, shares, "I was overjoyed and petrified when I found out my book was being published. Every writer's dream is to get a book published, but this one was going to show people what was really in my head, how I felt, what I did. I careened between happiness and nausea. I lost some friends when my book was published. But ripping my mask off turned out to be a massive relief. The more real I get, the freer I am. I've always been grateful for my sobriety, not proud." Cindy House was amazed after publishing her book that so many people embraced her and her son and contacted her to say they loved her book and admired her honesty. She was surprised that "I was less affected than I originally thought I would be by outing myself in this way. It's left me feeling very free and no longer in hiding." Ellie Schoenberger, author of the One Crafty Mother Blog, founder of The Bubble Hour podcast and was featured on *The Oprah Winfrey Show*, reveals that "From day one, I felt as though sharing about my recovery held me accountable, helped educate those around me about what recovery was all about, and helped others know they aren't alone. When I started to garner national attention for speaking publicly about recovery (a decade ago), there was some negative feedback from within the self-help community, which I wasn't prepared for . . . These days, with so many more people being open about recovery, I don't think this path is as hard as it was a decade ago."

PIRs choose different approaches to self-disclosure, finding one that feels comfortable for them. The intention behind either decision should be objectively examined. Sharing can provide more opportunities for PIRs to talk about their successes. However, the call to action is not for everyone, and it is essential to recognize how disclosure may impact individuals in various domains of their lives.

- "I just think that for a number of years, as long as I kept my past hidden, I felt split, like I wasn't living my life authentically. It's hard to live with secrets." —Cathy
- "The few people I have shared about being in recovery with are shocked as I am not what they think of." —Laura
- "When I am offered drinks or conversations about drinking arise, I have no problem telling people I am a person in recovery. That doesn't mean that I share all the details of my active addiction with everyone I come across, but I do not feel I have to hide the fact that I am an alcoholic." —Jackie
- "I don't talk about what self-help program I am in, but I am vocal about being in recovery. I do it to reduce the stigma, 'I am in long-term recovery.'" —Douglas
- "I tell everyone I meet I am in recovery. So, if they ever need help, they know they can call me." —Chase
- "I have become increasingly more vocal over the years." —Chris
- "I typically do not disclose I am in recovery at work or to the parents of my child's friends. I do not know their experience with recovery, and not everyone is excited about someone being in recovery if they have an addict in their life that has caused harm. I only disclose as appropriate if it will be helpful." —Cassie
- "Being honest has helped me. Secrets fueled my shame and guilt in active alcoholism, so it was important not to have secrets anymore. Transparency with my kids and family members was a key part of

taking accountability. Once I was more open about my alcoholism, the shame didn't feel as deep." —Tracie

- "Working on being proud of being in recovery was a good antidote to healing the shame of addiction. Not at the expense of cleaning up my wreckage, which is a personal thing, but as a way to show others it's possible, be a good example for my kids and even hold myself accountable." —Evelyn
- "Until I feel comfortable enough with someone, I will not share my story." —Violet
- "I don't usually disclose that I am in recovery. I will openly tell people I don't drink if it comes up. If they ask why, I usually just say 'for my health' or 'alcohol and I don't mix well.'" —Stacie
- "I am willing to disclose my recovery to those who would benefit from it. I don't disclose that I am in recovery as a general matter of discussion or recognition." —Marilyn
- "I tend to reveal that I am in recovery only to those whom I have grown comfortable with. If necessary, I tell people I am sober." —Mason
- "I am very open that I am in recovery and also am open at work (in addiction treatment). I feel a great amount of pride." —Steve
- "I tell everyone. I talk about it so much that I am sure people get bored with it. I take great pride in my sobriety this time and am very protective of it." —Rebecca

Transformation

PIRs and others in recovery are dynamic, intelligent, and driven individuals. While they lost their way and misdirected their attention and gifts toward obtaining and using substances, recovery frees them to contribute to society in ways they were meant to. Research by Jason Roop, PhD, has found that those with SUDs have unique leadership and positive qualities that produce organizational and societal benefits once they enter recovery. Some common traits identified were "tenacity, resilience, empathy, authenticity, motivational, self-awareness, creativity, social intelligence, determination and appreciation."[16] While these traits may have been previously used to maintain their addiction, through their hard work in the treatment process, individuals can shift their application toward empowerment. PIRs and others can mold their buried talents to add meaning and purpose to their lives. This understanding can be another way to break the stereotype with real-life examples of recovery success.[17] While an active SUD negatively impacts every life domain, recovery has the contrasting ability to positively impact each area. Recovery does not limit individuals to settle for mediocrity. Instead, it means they have a drive and resiliency that supersedes those of the average person.

Many PIRs credit some form of spirituality for their sobriety or even for saving their lives. One misconception is that religion and spirituality are intended or designed for those who have behaved in perfect or conformist ways. Some PIRs raised with religious backgrounds report their association with God or a higher power as one of fear or of an idea that was pushed upon them. However, "God comes through the wound"[18] and "The spirituality of imperfection is the spirituality of the weak and the broken, the poor and the humble. It is and always has been a spirituality for people with large and strong passions, with troubled pasts and uncertain futures, a spirituality both ordinary and unconventional."[19] The relationship that PIRs have with God or a higher power may initially begin with feelings of abandonment or a lack of worthiness. Violet describes this evolution, stating, "In my early recovery, I came in with an extremely negative viewpoint on everything that resembled 'higher power.' I wanted nothing to do with one. My belief at the time was that 'God' had failed me in many ways, including him being punishing . . . Working through my resentments toward 'this God,' and researching deities and other spiritual practices, I find things that resonate with my soul and leave me feeling connected and energized." Those in recovery often begin to accept their past and recognize that they have been given a second chance to thrive. Evelyn describes her conception of spirituality as knowing that she was "not the be all and end all of everything that happens—good or bad." She also found that "tapping into the energy of a room full of recovering people was a kind of spirituality." This open interpretation of spirituality has been healing for many—allowing for connection and self-forgiveness. "The goal of this particular journey known as life is not to prove that we are perfect but to find some happiness, some joyful peace of mind in the reality of our own imperfection."[20]

PIRs spoke openly about their gratitude and even amazement at their evolution since getting sober. That single choice forever shifted the trajectory of their lives and has allowed them to be responsible and loving parents—reconnecting with their inner compass. The recovery journey is never over and involves an ongoing process, like peeling back the layers of an onion, with countless growth opportunities. PIRs are role models for their children through their perseverance, vulnerability, and humanness, which contrasts the parental ideal they may have previously held of flawlessness, control, and invincibility.

The Recovery Pride Movement

Throughout history, social health movements have begun with secrecy and stigma and evolved over time into advocacy and hope. Examples include HIV/AIDS, postpartum depression, breast cancer, physical disabilities, and more. The only way that these movements occurred was because affected individuals, families, and allies dared to step forward, tell their stories, and push for change. With more than 100 million people in America affected by addiction, the need continues to shift the narrative and focus to *how* individuals can recover and support each other.[21] William White explains the importance of humanizing a condition, stating, "I can give you all the facts. I can read all the books to you. I can show you documentaries. But nothing's going to change that embedded prejudice until you personally encounter someone in recovery who means something to you and hear his or her story. When we ask people how their attitudes have changed related to addiction and the prospects of recovery, the most powerful ingredient in their change is that they know someone in recovery, within their own family or their own social or occupational network."[22]

Addiction treatment professionals have observed a positive shift in the recovery pride movement over many years. Susan Berlin is hopeful and discloses, "I do see more folks feeling prideful of their recovery. I give anyone permission to tell people that I have been sober for nearly 35 years. So, I model the pride version of this, and I talk about how much my life has improved and that all the ways I struggled while using are so diminished now if they exist at all. I also see social media, TV, etc., that involve recovery and the positive ways life changes when in recovery, and that is so exciting to see." Jill Griffin, LICSW, LADC, offers insight, stating, "It is more common to be in recovery and be open about it today due to social media and other forms of celebration of sobriety in general. I have seen a shift in my own time being sober about how people feel more comfortable discussing the fact that they chose not to drink or use drugs anymore." Jennifer Barba has seen, "The recovery pride movement has gained momentum, fostering a more positive and empowering perspective on the recovery journey. It encourages individuals in recovery to embrace their sobriety and to be proud of the positive changes they have made in their lives. One of the notable changes I have observed is the increased visibility and openness surrounding recovery. More individuals are sharing their stories of recovery, breaking the silence and stigma associated with addiction. This openness has created a sense of community and support, allowing people to feel less alone and more encouraged to seek help." Dan Lynch has observed, "There appears to be more awareness, especially through social media platforms. There are mocktails at events and also sober parties. There is less judgment and a sense of understanding and support. There is this movement of 'if you are doing something healthy, then we are all for it.'"

PIRs who chose to break their silence publicly have been on the receiving end of encouraging feedback from readers and listeners. Brenda Wilhelmson shares that most of the feedback she receives from readers is to "thank me for writing that book because my story mirrors theirs . . . My readers have a lot of hope. They are relieved to know that there is a way out, and they want out." Ellie Schoenberger adds, "Now, I'm *never* sheepish or small about being in recovery. I have never experienced one moment of shame about being a woman and a parent in recovery. I believe with my whole heart that by speaking openly about recovery, we are helping countless people—even when we don't know we are."

Large-scale national events have also gained traction, including National Recovery Month, which started in 1989 and is held every September "to promote and support new evidence-based treatment and recovery practices, the nation's strong and proud recovery community, and the dedication of service providers and communities who make recovery in all its forms possible."[23] The "Walk for Recovery," "Shatterproof Walk," "Changing the Face of Addiction," and other such events have attracted large numbers of participants and allow for the same type of support and visibility as the runs and walks for more prominent causes such as multiple sclerosis, cancer, autism, and other conditions. In addition, many new online self-help recovery communities evolved before the COVID-19 pandemic and some as a result of it. These communities have an abstinence-based, moderation management, harm reduction, and "sober curious" philosophy—attracting many individuals who may have otherwise been turned off. The sober curious movement comprises individuals who have felt the negative impact of alcohol and substance use in their lives but do not necessarily meet the criteria for an SUD or are not ready to commit fully to an abstinence-based group. The movement has also lent itself to more positive associations with the sober lifestyle, as well as making it more socially acceptable and even desirable. Jennifer Barba puts these changes into context, stating, "The emergence of the 'Sober Curious' movement has played a role in the shift toward recovery pride. It has sparked curiosity and encouraged individuals to explore a sober lifestyle even if they do not identify as having a substance use disorder. This movement has promoted a more mindful and intentional approach to alcohol and substance use, fostering a culture of self-reflection and healthier choices." However, with ongoing advocacy and societal shifts, PIRs and other individuals in recovery can still experience misunderstanding, moral judgment, discrimination, stigma, and a lack of cohesive treatment options.

Recovery pride can be expressed on a larger and more public scale but also occurs interpersonally and within family systems. Dan Griffin, author of several books including *Amazing Dads! Fatherhood Curriculum* and featured in the movie *The Anonymous People*, has learned that some individuals choose not to share openly about their recovery beyond their self-help group because of shame. Others do not because "their experience of recovery is so sacred to them that they don't feel the need to take it out of the context in which they live it . . . They say they're being most helpful right here, right now—one-on-one with other men in recovery (in their self-help group)."[24] To this point, PIRs each have unique perspectives, and many have shifted their view as they have progressed into long-term recovery or as their immediate family system and even families of origin have been able to forgive and heal. Most reported that their family system has been very supportive through the years. Tracie comments that her family is very proud of her and shares these feelings with her. Cassie acknowledges that she feels the most pride in her family system because they are proud of her and celebrate her anniversaries. David describes his household as a "sober house with much pride in overcoming problems. This invites gratitude and unity." Laura recalls, "On my fifth sober anniversary, my sister brought me roses. My dad's last words to me were that he is so proud of me. My younger son has shared with his friends as needed about my recovery, in fact, he brought one to his first meeting." Mason notes that his family of origin struggles with SUDs, but they "are so proud of my sobriety. The few that are coherent enough to realize it anyway." Marilyn shares that her adult children "are proud that I am in recovery, and they share this fact with their friends." Steve appreciates others' curiosity about his recovery and answers questions they may have because many know someone else who has also struggled. Sharon reveals that friends and family can see the dignity in how she lives her life and in sharing her story, commenting, "My children tell me how proud they are of the woman I have become since getting sober." Violet shares that she and her family celebrate her recovery with dinners, cards, and balloons each year.

Evelyn had challenges with her family of origin, revealing, "My mom, in particular, really struggled with how I could feel proud about being in recovery. As time went on, however, she worked on being able to understand more about addiction and recovery, and she totally jumped on the 'wave the flag' bandwagon and talked openly with others about my recovery. But, after my relapse, she really struggled. She thought recovery was a 'one and done' type of thing, and she was really hurt and angry when I relapsed. That took a long time to repair." However, within her immediate family system, "My kids speak openly about it (with my permission), and their friends have even come to me for help." Chris adds that his immediate family supports him and even attends self-help meetings with him. However, to this day, his family of origin struggles to understand his recovery.

Nevertheless, some PIRs do not allow for much praise around their recovery. They feel that this can be viewed as lacking the modesty they need to maintain sobriety and not become complacent. Douglas shares, "Pride can lack humility, and I avoid that at times." Cathy struggles to accept praise around her recovery. She mainly feels blessed to have survived and remained sober. However, a "Butterfly Effect" exists for all who touch one or a million lives with their story. That energy is transmitted to others and will continue to positively impact the recovery pride movement.

Parent Recovery Wisdom

> *"I aim to empower my clients to embrace their recovery with pride and self-compassion. By normalizing their experiences, reframing their narrative and celebrating their achievements, I help them recognize their strengths and resilience. Witnessing their transformation from a place of shame to one of pride is incredibly rewarding and inspires me to continue supporting them on their path to recovery."*
>
> —Jennifer Barba

The following strategies are from PIRs themselves and addiction treatment professionals. These approaches focus on shifting an individual's inner and outer narrative, developing shame resiliency, and fostering self-compassion. Some are listed exactly as stated by the PIRs to capture their tone and message. The following suggestions are meant to provide options and are not intended to be used in their entirety.

Shifting the Narrative

- Spend time with people who celebrate your recovery.
- When sharing your "story," focus on your recovery and what your life is like now and less on the wreckage of the past.
- Consider identifying as a "person in recovery" or "person in long-term recovery."
- Start sharing your story at self-help meetings to increase your sense of internal and external acceptance.
- Stand in conviction for who you are, a lot of people admire this.
- Share your experience of recovery with others.
- Join recovery pride events such as runs, walks, social events, fund-raisers.
- Connect with other PIRs about their level of recovery pride.
- Think about how you would want your child(ren) to perceive recovery and explore any discrepancies you may have.

Shame Resiliency

The following suggestions are opportunities to practice authenticity when you experience shame, move through the experience without sacrificing your values and find a new sense of strength.

Four key steps:

1. *Recognize shame and understand the triggers*: Can you physically recognize when you are in the grips of shame, feel your way through it, and figure out what messages and expectations prompted it?
2. *Practice critical awareness*: Can you reality-check the messages and expectations driving your shame? Are they realistic? Attainable? Are they what you want to be or what you think others need or want from you?
3. *Reach out*: Do you own and share your story? We can't experience empathy if we do not connect.
4. *Speak shame*: Do you talk about how you feel and ask for what you need when you feel shame?[25]

Other suggestions:

- Be aware that the "fight or flight" response is often set off and that our emotions hijack our thoughts.
- Repeat grounding words to regulate your emotions, such as "this too shall pass," "I am safe and all right in this moment," and so on.
- Recognize if you tend to "move toward" to please or "move against" to gain power in response to shame.
- Speak about how you feel only with individuals who have earned the right to hear it.
- Engage in self-talk as though you are supporting someone else who is feeling how you do.
- Own your story verbally or in writing and recognize that you have control over how to craft the ending.[26]
- Journal when you are in a place to find meaning around an event, but do not force the writing process.

Self-Compassion

Self-compassion involves acting the same way toward yourself that you would toward another person when having a difficult time, failing, or noticing character flaws. The deep awareness of one's suffering is accompanied by the wish to alleviate it.[27]

- Use imagery such as innocent beings (e.g., kittens, puppies, babies) to open your heart and picture caring for yourself as you would for them.
- "A moment of self-compassion can change your entire day. A string of such moments can change your whole life."[28]
- Be gentle with yourself so that you are more apt to reach out for support.
- Know that bringing kindness to ourselves is essential to inner warming with whatever experience is unfolding.
- Remember that you are not alone and that everyone suffers in some way.
- Engage in mindfulness of being here in this moment, just as you are.
- Remain aware of your five senses: taste, touch, smell, sound, and sight. Know that a slight shift in any can be grounding.
- Take self-compassion breaks throughout the day.
- Take in the good and fully absorb beneficial experiences.
- Place your hands on your heart when breathing deeply.
- Know that momentary states of nurturance can evolve into a trait of self-kindness.
- Find soothing mantras to repeat, such as "We are enough as we are," "We are loved," "We can love ourselves the way we want to be loved," and "May I be kind to myself."

Personal Journal Entries

March 14, 2006, Age 29, two years sober

I feel able to see beyond my own distorted thoughts around alcohol . . . My recovery program has helped me to challenge the distorted thoughts that alcoholism created within my mind.

Throughout my life struggles, I had some part of my soul connected to my future path. I prayed and waited for the time to come when I could look back on my pain and help others to cope. That time has finally come, and I have arrived here "one day at a time." I can finally look back on what was once me. I felt shame about the alcoholic part of my life and now I feel pride in sharing it with others. I felt fear about people knowing I am an alcoholic, but I now feel strength and liberation. I can honestly say that I have something to offer others—sobriety, wisdom, and serenity.

February 2, 2007, Age 30, three years sober

I got married, I am sober, I have a home, I am content . . . so much has changed . . . Through all the ups and downs, I have transcended with God as my guide. I am not perfect. I am still working on myself and falling at times—but I get back up with love and support.

Some of the pain of the past has scarred me—but the guilt has lifted. For today I see the truth—my truth . . . and the thing that I am most proud of is that I went "any length for my sobriety." My life has come a long way from my last drink, the bar and the blackout—by the grace of God.

There have been dramatic internal and external shifts in my life from early sobriety . . . and into longer-term recovery. I have emerged from the tunnel of early sobriety and am amazed at the clarity I now have regarding my alcoholism and how it has impacted my life and relationships. Recovery has allowed me to find my true self, and I have discovered my true self who was hidden behind the drinking, the socializing and the chaos of my addiction. I cannot compare my drinking life to my life in recovery—they feel like separate existences.

The growth process of recovery never ends. Just as one obstacle is faced and lessons are learned, another may arise. Though challenges constantly occur and uncomfortable feelings still crop up, they pass and I have the tools to get through them. I may be afraid at times, but I am always reassured that no matter what happens in my life, I will be alright—I have a source of power to tap into—God.[29]

In 2009, I made a choice to identify publicly as a woman in recovery with aspects of my story published in my book *Understanding the High-Functioning Alcoholic*, along with media appearances on TV, radio, podcasts, online, and print publications. My intention was always to change the face of alcoholism due to my own misconceptions that I knew were held by so many others. I, too, had felt embarrassed and uncomfortable admitting I was sober—sadly, more so than being in active addiction. However, throughout my recovery and healing process, with the help of family, friends, self-help groups, spirituality, and therapy, I have come to feel a sense of gratitude and pride surrounding my recovery, especially as a PIR. Openness about being a person in long-term recovery has allowed me to help others personally and professionally who otherwise may not have been reached. May the recovery movement continue to grow as PIRs and other individuals tell their stories, connect, and heal.

Resources

Self-Help Groups for Individuals with SUDs

- Alcoholics Anonymous (12-step spiritual): www.aa.org
- Celebrate Recovery (Christian): www.celebraterecovery.org
- Lifering Secular Recovery (Secular): www.lifering.org
- Narcotics Anonymous (12-step spiritual): www.na.org
- Recovery Dharma (Buddhist non-theistic): www.recoverydharma.org
- Recovery Yoga Meetings (all recovery, movement-based): www.yogameetings.com
- Secular AA (atheist, agnostic 12-step): www.aasecular.org
- Secular Organization for Sobriety (atheist, agnostic): www.sossobriety.org
- SHE RECOVERS (all recovery, trained facilitators): www.sherecovers.org
- SMART Recovery (cognitive behavioral skills-based): www.smartrecovery.org
- The Phoenix (adventure-based): www.thephoenix.org
- Women for Sobriety (spiritual): www.womenforsobriety.org

Self-Help Groups for Loved Ones

- Adult Children of Alcoholics: www.adultchildren.org
- Al-Anon and Al-Ateen Family Groups: www.al-anon.org

- Nar-Anon Family Groups: www.nar-anon.org
- SHE RECOVERS: www.sherecovers.org
- Learn 2 Cope: www.learn2cope.org
- C.A.R.E.S. Group: www.thecaresgroup.org

Self-Help Groups for Mental Health

- Depression and Bipolar Support Alliance (DBSA): www.dbsalliance.org
- NAMI Groups: www.nami.org/Support-Education/Support-Groups
- Postpartum Support International (PSI): www.postpartum.net

Alcohol Screening and Moderation Goal Setting:
NIAAA Rethinking Drinking: www.rethinkingdrinking.niaaa.nih.gov

General SUD and Treatment Information:
SAMHSA: www.samhsa.gov

Psychology Today provider finder with specializations listed:
www.psychologytoday.com/us/therapists

Suicide Helpline:
Call or text 988
www.988lifeline.org

Acknowledgments

TO JOSH AND EVE, you have given me the blessing of being a parent in recovery. I love you both beyond written words. I am so grateful for your patience with my writing process and for giving me the time and space I needed to complete this passion project.

To my mother, Jocelyn Allen, thank you for your unconditional love and support throughout my recovery journey and my career. Most of all, thank you for *not* editing my book. I love you.

To my father, Leo Allen, your belief that I could do *anything* is something I have internalized my entire life. This certainty has allowed me to write this book as well as my first, to push my own limits and to "go for it!" I love you.

To my editor Susan Aiello, you have been a gift in my life, with the talent to help me express my message in the most effective way. Your competence, sense of humor and knowledge gave me the confidence to press on and to know that I was on the right path.

To my publisher Rowman & Littlefield, thank you for giving me the opportunity to touch lives through my writing.

To my dear friend Tricia Anderson, you have always been my writing cheerleader. Once you have read my final book drafts, I feel certain that they are ready to launch into the world.

To my friend, colleague, and so much more, Jill Griffin, I respect your personal and professional opinion. Thank you for contributing to this book in so many meaningful ways.

Thank you to *each* of the PIRs I interviewed who had the courage to answer my probing questions and took the time to contribute. Your voices are the heart, the soul, and the life breath of this book. I was touched by your words and healed by your truths.

To the parents not in recovery who kindly responded to my survey, I thank you for your time and support. You added an important point of comparison and dimension to this book.

To Molly Ashcroft, Jennifer Barba, Susan Berlin, Nicole Castiglioni, Sheila Coleman, Margo Friedman, Cody Gardner, Victoria LaMadeleine, Dan Lynch, Elizabeth Modugno, Melany Montrond, Nancy Nitenson, and Vanessa Stanley, I am so grateful for your time and the insight your offered in your responses. This book is much richer because of your knowledge and years of experience working in the addiction treatment field.

To Brenda Wilhelmson, Rachel Brownell, and Ellie Schoenberger, I am so grateful to have connected with you as other mothers in recovery. Your strength to write and speak publicly about your experiences decreases stigma and opens the door for other parents.

To Cindy House, your book *Mother Noise* caught my eye in my local bookstore and planted a seed for this book. I appreciate your vulnerability and willingness to share your story so brilliantly, as well as being part of my book—a true honor.

To all of my wise, unique, and fierce friends in recovery—you have each touched my life in ways that are reflected in this book, thank you.

To the millions of PIRs, thank you for your bravery—your stories matter. You are all an inspiration to your children, to your loved ones and to the world.

To the millions of parents with substance use disorders who have not been able to get help or who have struggled to recover: may you reach out for support, know you are *not* alone and have faith that recovery is possible.

Notes

Introduction

1. U.S. Department of Health and Human Services (HHS), Substance Abuse and Mental Health Services Administration (SAMHSA), "SAMHSA Announces National Survey on Drug Use and Health (NSDUH) Results Detailing Mental Illness and Substance Use Levels in 2021," hhs.gov, https://www.hhs.gov/about/news/2023/01/04/samhsa-announces-national-survey-drug-use-health-results-detailing-mental-illness-substance-use-levels-2021.html (accessed May 15, 2023).
2. Ibid.
3. U.S. Census Bureau, "Families and Living Arrangements: 2020," last modified September 15, 2021, https://www.census.gov/data/tables/2020/demo/families/cps-2020.html (accessed May 15, 2023).
4. R. N. Lipari and S. L. Van Horn, "Children Living with Parents Who Have a Substance Use Disorder," The CBHSQ Report: August 24, 2017 (Rockville, MD: Substance Abuse and Mental Health Services Administration, Center for Behavioral Health Statistics and Quality, 2017).
5. U.S. Department of Health and Human Services (HHS), Substance Abuse and Mental Health Services Administration (SAMHSA), "SAMHSA Announces National Survey on Drug Use and Health (NSDUH) Results Detailing Mental Illness and Substance Use Levels in 2021," hhs.gov, https://www.hhs.gov/about/news/2023/01/04/samhsa-announces-national-survey-drug-use-health-results-detailing-mental-illness-substance-use-levels-2021.html (accessed May 15, 2023).

Chapter 1: Recovery as a Lifestyle

1. J. F. Kelly et al., "Prevalence and Pathways of Recovery from Drug and Alcohol Problems in the United States Population: Implications for Practice, Research, and Policy," *Drug Alcohol Depend* 181, no. Supplement C (2017): 162–69, https://doi.org/10.1016/j.drugalcdep.2017.09.028.

2. Substance Abuse and Mental Health Services Administration, "Recovery and Recovery Support," accessed May 10, 2023, https://www.samhsa.gov/find-help/recovery.

3. J. Jorquez, "The Retirement Phase of Heroin Using Careers," *Journal of Drug Issues* 18, no. 3 (1983): 343–65.

4. Connecticut Community for Addiction Recovery, *Recovery Coach Academy* curriculum (2015): 100–3.

5. Ibid., 51–52.

6. Merriam-Webster Dictionary, "Lifestyle," accessed May 11, 2023, https://www.merriam-webster.com/dictionary/lifestyle.

7. Bud Mikhitarian, *Many Faces, One Voice: Secrets from The Anonymous People* (Las Vegas: Central Recovery Press, 2015), 31.

8. Ibid., 106–7.

9. Merriam-Webster Dictionary, "Imposter Syndrome," accessed May 16, 2023, https://www.merriam-webster.com/dictionary/impostor%20syndrome.

Chapter 2: The Intrinsic and Extrinsic Parenting Continuum

1. Jennifer Senior, *All Joy and No Fun: The Paradox of Modern Parenthood* (New York: HarperCollins, 1994), 3.

2. D. Baumrind, "Current Patterns of Parental Authority," *Developmental Psychology* 4, no. 1 (1971): 103, https://doi: 10.1037/h0030372.

3. D. Baumrind, "The Influence of Parenting Style on Adolescent Competence and Substance Abuse," The *Journal of Early Adolescence* No. 11(1991): 56–95, https://doi:10.1177/0272431691111004.

4. S. Kuppens and E. Ceulemans, "Parenting Styles: A Closer Look at a Well-Known Concept," *Journal of Child and Family Studies* 28, no. 1 (2019):168–81, doi: 10.1007/s10826-018-1242-x.

5. Jessica Grose, *Screaming on the Inside: The Unsustainability of American Motherhood* (New York: Mariner Books, 2022): 110–11.

6. Ibid., book jacket.

7. K. Gill, "Maternal Instinct: Does it Really Exist?," accessed June 1, 2023, https://www.healthline.com/health/parenting/maternal-instinct#is-it-a-myth.

8. American Society for Reproductive Medicine, "Waiting to Have a Baby? Don't Wait Too Long," accessed July 26, 2023, https://www.reproductivefacts.org/news-and-publications/fact-sheets-and-infographics.

9. K. Gill, "Maternal Instinct."

10. Ibid.

11. Lixia Qu and Ruth Weston, "Opinions of Parents on the Acquisition of Parenting and Relationship Skills," *Family Matters: Australian Institute of Family Studies* 81 (2009): 55–57.

12. I. Røseth, R. Bongaardt, A. Lyberg, E. Sommerseth, and B. Dahl, "New Mothers' Struggles to Love Their Child: An Interpretative Synthesis of Qualitative Studies," *International Journal of Qualitative Studies on Health and Well-being* 13, no. 1 (December 2018):1490621, https://doi: 10.1080/17482631.2018.1490621., quoted in Karen Gill, "Maternal Instinct."

13. L. A. Lebrun-Harris, R. M. Ghandour, M. D. Kogan, and M. D. Warren, "Five-Year Trends in US Children's Health and Well-being, 2016–2020," *JAMA Pediatrics* 176, no. 7 (2022), https://doi:10.1001/jamapediatrics.2022.0056.

Chapter 3: Family, Marriage, and Partnership

1. Kahlil Gibran, *The Prophet* (New York: Knopf, 1923, Project Gutenburg, January 1, 2019), https://www.gutenberg.org/cache/epub/58585/pg58585-images.html#link19.

2. Study.com, "Family Systems: Types, Benefits and Examples," accessed June 8, 2023), https://study.com/learn/lesson/family-system-types-examples.html.

3. Michael Nichols and Richard Schwartz, *Family Therapy: Concepts and Methods* (Boston: Pearson Education Company, 2001), 137–38.

4. Amy Marschall, "What Is Bowenian Family Therapy?," accessed June 8, 2023, https://www.verywellmind.com/bowenian-family-therapy-definition-and-techniques-5214558.

5. L. Lander, J. Howsare, and M. Byrne, "The Impact of Substance Use Disorders on Families and Children: From Theory to Practice," *Social Work in Public Health* 28, no. 3–4 (2013): 194–205, https://doi: 10.1080/19371918.2013.759005.

6. Ibid.

7. National Institute of Health, National Institute of Alcohol Abuse and Alcoholism, "Genetics of Alcohol Use Disorder," accessed June 9, 2023, https://www.niaaa.nih.gov/alcohols-effects-health/alcohol-use-disorder/genetics-alcohol-use-disorder.

8. J. D. Deak and E. C. Johnson, "Genetics of Substance Use Disorders: A Review," *Psychological Medicine* 51, No. 13 (October 2021): 2189–2200, https://doi: 10.1017/S0033291721000969.

9. National Institute of Health, "Genetics of Alcohol Use Disorder."

10. J. D. Deak, "Genetics of Substance Use Disorders."

11. L. Lander, J. Howsare, and M. Byrne, "The Impact of Substance Use Disorders on Families and Children."

12. Ibid.

13. Brian D. Doss et al., "The Effect of the Transition to Parenthood on Relationship Quality: An Eight-Year Prospective Study," *Journal of Personality and Social Psychology* 96, no. 3 (2009): 601–19.

14. J. M. Twenge, W. K. Campbell, and C. A. Foster, "Parenthood and Marital Satisfaction: A Meta-analytic Review," *Journal of Marriage and Family* 65, no. 3 (2003): 574–83.

15. T. J. O'Farrell and K. Clements, "Review of Outcome Research on Marital and Family Therapy in Treatment for Alcoholism," *Journal of Marital and Family Therapy 38*, no. 1 (2012): 122–44, https://doi:10.1111/j.1752-0606.2011.00242.

16. V. E. Horigian et al., "Long-Term Effects of Brief Strategic Family Therapy for Adolescent Substance Users," *Drug and Alcohol Dependence Journal*, 140 (2014), e91.

17. S. Bartle-Haring, N. Slesnick, and A. Murnan, "Benefits to Children Who Participate in Family Therapy with Their Substance-Using Mother," *Journal of Marital Family Therapy 44*, no. 4 (2018): 671–86, https://doi:10.1111/jmft.12280.

18. Melody Beattie, *Codependent No More* (Center City, MN: Hazelden Press, 1992): 36.

19. Ibid., 62.

20. Ibid., 57.

21. Robert Meyers and Brenda Wolfe, *Get Your Loved One Sober: Alternatives to Nagging, Pleading, and Threatening* (Center City, MN: Hazelden Publishing, 2004).

22. Bud Mikhitarian, *Many Faces, One Voice: Secrets from The Anonymous People* (Las Vegas: Central Recovery Press, 2015), 284–85.

23. Diana Clark, *Family Healing Strategies* workbook (Self-Published, 2008), 22.

24. Ibid.

25. S. Brown et al., "Personal Network Recovery Enablers and Relapse Risks for Women with Substance Dependence," *Qualitative Health Research 25*, no. 3 (2015): 371–85, https://doi:10.1177/1049732314551055, quoted in Substance Abuse and Mental Health Services Administration. "Substance Use Disorder Treatment and Family Therapy," *Treatment Improvement Protocol (TIP) Series No. 39* (Rockville, MD: Substance Abuse and Mental Health Services Administration, 2020), 9.

Chapter 4: Get a Life

1. U.S. Bureau of Labor Statistics, "Women in the Labor Force: A Databook," accessed July 10, 2023, https://www.bls.gov/cps/cps_over.htm.
2. Ibid.
3. Ibid.
4. Merriam-Webster Dictionary, "Identity," accessed July 11, 2023, https://www.merriam-webster.com/dictionary/identity.
5. Jessica Valenti, *Why Have Kids*, 98.
6. Rachel Brownell, *Mommy Doesn't Drink Here Anymore* (San Francisco, CA: Conari Press, 2009): 19.
7. Ibid., 58.
8. Trish Elizabeth, "Around the Carousel" (Unpublished manuscript with permission): 43–59.
9. Jeff Szymanski, *The Perfectionist's Handbook: Take Risks, Invite Criticism, and Make the Most of Your Mistakes* (Hoboken, NJ: Harvard Health Publications, 2011): 5–11.
10. Jessica Valenti, *Why Have Kids*, 69.
11. Ibid., 70.
12. Rosemary O'Connor, *A Sober Mom's Guide to Recovery* (Center City, MN: Hazelden Press, 2015): 78.

Chapter 5: Self-Care Is Not Optional

1. Merriam-Webster Dictionary, "Self-Care," accessed May 23, 2023, https://www.merriam-webster.com/dictionary/self-care.
2. N. Martínez et al., "Self-Care: A Concept Analysis," *International Journal of Nursing Science* 8, no. 4 (2021): 418–25.
3. Ibid.
4. Chrissy King, "Self-Care Is an Act of Survival," accessed May 25, 2023, https://www.girlsgonestrong.com/blog/articles/self-care-act-survival/.
5. Ibid.
6. Edward Khantzian and Mark Albanese, "The Self-Medication Hypothesis of Substance Use Disorders: A Reconsideration and Recent Application," *Harvard Review of Psychiatry* 4, no. 5 (1997): 231–44.
7. Edward Khantzian and Mark Albanese, *Understanding Addiction as Self-Medication* (Lanham, MD: Rowman and Littlefield, 2008), 19–20.
8. Jennifer Senior, *All Joy and No Fun: The Paradox of Modern Parenting* (New York: HarperCollins, 2014), 126.
9. Chrissy King, "Self-Care Is an Act of Survival."

Chapter 6: Coping with Hard Times

1. Merriam-Webster Dictionary, "Stress." accessed on May 25, 2023, https://www.merriam-webster.com/dictionary/stress.

2. Rob Cross and Karen Dillon, "The Hidden Toll of Microstress," *Harvard Business Review,* accessed February 7, 2023, https://hbr.org/2023/02/the-hidden-toll-of-microstress.

3. Ibid.

4. Herbert Benson and Eileen M. Stuart, *The Wellness Book: The Comprehensive Guide to Maintaining and Treating Stress-Related Illness* (New York: A Fireside Book, 1992).

5. National Institute of Health, National Institute on Alcohol Abuse and Alcoholism, "The Link Between Stress and Alcohol," *Alcohol Alert* no. 8 (2012): 3–4.

6. Rosemary O'Connor, *A Sober Mom's Guide to Recovery* (Center City, MN: Hazelden Press, 2015), 55.

7. Ibid.

8. Trish Elizabeth, "Around the Carousel," unpublished manuscript, 52.

9. Ibid., 109.

10. D. Cucinotta and M. Vanelli, "WHO Declares COVID-19 a Pandemic." *Acta Biomedica* 91, no. 1 (March 19, 2020):157–60, https://doi: 10.23750/abm.v91i1.9397.

11. Center for Disease Control and Prevention, "End of Federal COVID-19 Public Health Emergency (PHE) Declaration," accessed May 5, 2023, https://www.cdc.gov/coronavirus/2019-ncov/your-health/end-of-phe.html#:~:text=May%2011%2C%202023%2C%20marks%20the,to%20the%20COVID%2D19%20pandemic.

12. M. É. Czeisler et al., "Mental Health, Substance Use, and Suicidal Ideation During the COVID-19 Pandemic—United States, June 24–30, 2020," *MMWR Morbidity and Mortality Weekly Report* 69 (2020):1049-1057, http://dx.doi.org/10.15585/mmwr.mm6932a1external icon.

13. American Psychological Association, "Stress in the Time of COVID-19," *Stress in America,* May 2020, vol. 1, https://www.apa.org/news/press/releases/stress/2020/report.

14. Ibid.

15. Nirmita Panchal et al., "The Implications of COVID-19 for Mental Health and Substance Use," *Kaiser Family Foundation Issues Brief,* updated February 10, 2021, https://www.kff.org/coronavirus-covid-19/issue-brief/the-implications-of-covid-19-for-mental-health-and-substance-use/.

16. M. S. Pollard, J. S. Tucker, and H. D. Green, "Changes in Adult Alcohol Use and Consequences During the COVID-19 Pandemic in the US," *Journal*

of the American Medical Association Network Open 3, no. 9 (2020): https://doi:10.1001/jamanetworkopen.2020.22942.

17. Panchal, "The Implications of COVID-19," updated February 10, 2021.

18. C. K. Ettman et al., "Persistent Depressive Symptoms During COVID-19: A National, Population-Representative, Longitudinal Study of U.S. Adults," *The Lancet Regional Health- Americas* 5 (2022), https://doi.org/10.1016/j.lana.2021.100091.

19. Panchal, "The Implications of COVID-19," updated March 20, 2023.

20. Ibid.

21. E. P. Terlizza and J. S. Schiller, "Estimates of Mental Health Symptomatology, by Month of Interview: United States, 2019," *National Center for Health Statistics*, March 2021.

22. Jessica Grose, *Screaming on the Inside: The Unsustainability of American Motherhood* (New York: Mariner Books, 2022), 152.

Chapter 7: Staying Sane

1. Substance Abuse and Mental Health Services Administration, *Key Substance Use and Mental Health Indicators in the United States: Results from the 2020 National Survey on Drug Use and Health* (Rockville, MD: Center for Behavioral Health Statistics and Quality, Substance Abuse and Mental Health Services Administration, 2021), 3, https://www.samhsa.gov/data/release/2021-national-survey-drug-use-and-health-nsduh-releases.

2. Ibid.

3. R. H. Pietrzak, R. B. Goldstein, S. M. Southwick, and B. F. Grant, "Prevalence and Axis I Comorbidity of Full and Partial Posttraumatic Stress Disorder in the United States: Results from Wave 2 of the National Epidemiologic Survey on Alcohol and Related Condition," *Journal of Anxiety Disorders 25* (2011): 456–65, https://doi:10.1016/j.janxdis.2010.11.010.

4. R. C. Kessler, L. Adler, R. Barkley et al. "The Prevalence and Correlates of Adult ADHD in the United States: Results from the National Comorbidity Survey Replication," *American Journal of Psychiatry* 163 (2006):716–23.

5. B. F. Grant and D. A. Dawson, "Age at Onset of Alcohol Use and Its Association with DSM-IV Alcohol Abuse and Dependence: Results from the National Longitudinal Alcohol Epidemiologic Survey," *Journal of Substance Abuse* 9 (1997):103–10.

6. Substance Abuse and Mental Health Services Administration, *Results from the 2013 National Survey*, 85.

7. Substance Abuse and Mental Health Services Administration, *Results from the 2013 National Survey on Drug Use and Health: Summary of National*

Findings (Rockville, MD: Substance Abuse and Mental Health Services Administration: 2014), 85.

8. B. F. Grant and D. A. Dawson, "Age at Onset of Alcohol Use," 103–10.

9. Substance Abuse and Mental Health Services Administration, *Behavioral Health Trends in the United States: Results from the 2014 National Survey on Drug Use and Health* (Rockville, MD: Center for Behavioral Health Statistics and Quality, Substance Abuse and Mental Health Services Administration, 2015), https://www.samhsa.gov/data/sites/default/files/NSDUH-FRR1-2014/NSDUH-FRR1-2014.pdf.

10. Substance Abuse and Mental Health Services Administration, "Age of Substance Use Initiation among Treatment Admissions Aged 18-30," *The TEDs Report*, July 17, 2014, https://www.samhsa.gov/data/sites/default/files/WebFiles_TEDS_SR142_AgeatInit_07-10-14/TEDS-SR142-AgeatInit-2014.htm.

11. National Institute of Health, National Institute on Drug Abuse, "Common Comorbidities with Substance Use Disorders Research Report, Part 1: The Connection between Substance Use Disorders and Mental Illness," accessed August 1, 2023, https://nida.nih.gov/publications/research-reports/common-*comorbiditie4.s*-substance-use-disorders/part-1-connection-between-substance-use-disorders-mental-illness.

12. National Sleep Foundation, "2004 Sleep in America Poll: Children and Sleep," accessed May 6, 2013, https://www.thensf.org/sleep-in-america-polls/, quoted in Jennifer Senior, *All Joy and No Fun: The Paradox of Modern Parenting* (New York: HarperCollins, 2014), 22.

13. Ibid.

14. Ibid., 21.

15. A. Divine, C. Blanchard, C. Benoit, D. S. Downs, and R. E. Rhodes, "The Influence of Sleep and Movement on Mental Health and Life Satisfaction during the Transition to Parenthood," *Sleep Health* 8, no. 5 (2022): 475–83, https://doi.org/10.1016/j.sleh.2022.06.013.

16. Columbia University Department of Psychiatry, "How Sleep Deprivation Impacts Mental Health," updated August 2, 2023, https://www.columbiapsychiatry.org/news/how-sleep-deprivation-affects-your-mental-health.

17. Bessel Van der Kolk, *The Body Keeps Score: Brain, Mind, and Body in the Healing of Trauma* (New York: Viking, 2014).

18. T. H. Rosenström and F. A. Torvik, "Social Anxiety Disorder Is a Risk Factor for Alcohol Use Problems in the National Comorbidity Surveys," *Drug and Alcohol Dependence* 1, no. 249 (August 2023), https://doi:10.1016/j.drugalcdep.2023.109945.

19. Substance Abuse and Mental Health Services Administration, *Key Substance Use and Mental Health Indicators in the United States*, 5.

20. Roger Weiss and Hilary Smith Connery, *Integrated Groups Therapy for Bipolar Disorder and Substance Abuse* (New York: Guilford Press, 2011).

21. Bill Wilson, "Emotional Sobriety," accessed August 4, 2023, https://barricks.com/AASayings/emotional.html.

22. Tian Dayton, *Emotional Sobriety: From Relationship Trauma to Resilience and Balance* (Deerfield Beach, FL: Health Communication, Inc., 2007), 1–2.

23. Substance Abuse and Mental Health Services Administration, *Key Substance Use and Mental Health Indicators*, 64–65.

24. Tian Dayton, *Emotional Sobriety*, 12–13.

25. Eckhart Tolle, *The Power of Now: A Guide to Spiritual Enlightenment* (Novato, CA: New World Library, 1999), 11–32.

26. Alcoholics Anonymous World Services, Inc., *Daily Reflections* (New York: Simon & Schuster, 1990), 109.

Chapter 8: The Dog Years

1. Rachel Minkin and Juliana Menasce Horowitz, *Parenting in America Today: A Survey Report (2023)* Pew Research Center, accessed August 22, 2023, https://www.pewresearch.org/social-trends/2023/01/24/parenting-in-america-today/.

2. Rachel Brownell, *Mommy Doesn't Drink Here Anymore* (San Francisco, CA: Conari Press, 2009), 44.

3. Center for Disease Control and Prevention, "Depression During and After Pregnancy," accessed August 24, 2023, https://www.cdc.gov/reproductivehealth/features/maternal-depression/.

4. K. L. Wisner et al., "Onset Timing, Thoughts of Self-Harm, and Diagnoses in Postpartum Women with Screen-Positive Depression Findings," *JAMA Psychiatry* 70, no. 5 (May 2013): 490–98. doi: 10.1001/jamapsychiatry.2013.87.

5. Jaydee Graham, *The Soul Grind* (Los Angeles: Launch Pad Publishing, 2021), 140.

6. Jessica Grose, *Screaming on the Inside: The Unsustainability of American Motherhood* (New York: Mariner Books, 2022), 53.

7. Ibid., 1–2.

8. L. S. Cohen, L. L. Altshuler, B. L. Harlow et al., "Relapse of Major Depression During Pregnancy in Women Who Maintain or Discontinue Antidepressant Treatment," *Journal of the American Medical Association* 295, no. 5 (2006):499–507, https://doi:10.1001/jama.295.5.499.

9. Jessica Grose, *Screaming on the Inside*, 2.

10. Jennifer Senior, *All Joy and No Fun: The Paradox of Modern Parenting* (New York: HarperCollins, 2014), 17.

11. Rachel Minkin and Juliana Menasce Horowitz, *Parenting in America Today*, accessed August 23, 2023, https://www.pewresearch.org/social-trends/2023/01/24/parenting-in-america-today/.

12. Center for Disease Control and Prevention, "Depression During and After Pregnancy," accessed August 24, 2023, https://www.cdc.gov/reproductivehealth/features/maternal-depression/.

13. J. F. Paulson and S. D. Bazemore, "Prenatal and Postpartum Depression in Fathers and its Association with Maternal Depression: A Meta-Analysis," *Journal of the American Medical Association* 303, no. 19 (May 2010): 1961–1969, https://doi:10.1001/jama.2010.605.

14. L. S. Leach, C. Poyser, A. R. Cooklin, and R. Giallo, "Prevalence and Course of Anxiety Disorders (and Symptom Levels) in Men Across the Perinatal Period: A Systematic Review," *Journal of Affective Disorders* 190 (Jan 2016): 675–86.

15. D. E. Saxbe et al. "Fathers' Decline in Testosterone and Synchrony with Partner Testosterone During Pregnancy Predicts Greater Postpartum Relationship Investment," *Hormones and Behavior* 90 (April 2017) 39–47. doi: 10.1016/j.yhbeh.2016.07.005.

16. Jessica Valenti, *Why Have Kids: A New Mom Explores the Truth About Parenting and Happiness* (New York: New Harvest Houghton Mifflin Harcourt, 2012), 98.

17. Jennifer Senior, *All Joy and No Fun*, 28.

18. Mihaly Csikszentmihalyi, *Flow: The Psychology of Optimal Experience* (New York: Harper-Perennial, 1991).

19. Jennifer Senior, *All Joy and No Fun*, 30.

20. Ibid., 32.

21. Ibid., 198.

22. S. S. Luthar and L. Ciciolla, "What it Feels Like to Be a Mother: Variations by Children's Developmental Stages," *Developmental Psychology* 52, no. 1 (January 2016):143–54, https://doi:10.1037/dev0000062.

23. Jennifer Senior, *All Joy and No Fun*, 199.

24. Cindy House, *Mother Noise* (New York: Marysue Rucci Books/Scribner, 2022), 1–7.

Chapter 9: Buzzkill

1. T. Morgan, N. Uomini, L. Rendell et al., "Experimental Evidence for the Co-Evolution of Hominin Tool-Making Teaching and Language," *Nature Communications* 6, no. 6029 (2015), https://doi.org/10.1038/ncomms7029.

2. Maria Cohut, *Medical News Today*, accessed September 5, 2023, https://www.medicalnewstoday.com/articles/what-are-the-health-benefits-of-friendship#Connection-matters,-but-its-not-about-numbers.

3. Ibid.

4. J. Holt-Lunstad, T. B. Smith, and J. B. Layton, "Social Relationships and Mortality Risk: A Meta-analytic Review," *PLOS Medicine* 7, no. 7 (2010), e1000316. https://doi.org/10.1371/journal.pmed.1000316.

5. D. Umberson and J. K. Montez, "Social Relationships and Health: A Flashpoint for Health Policy," *Journal of Health and Social Behavior* 51 Supplement (2010): S54–66, https://doi: 10.1177/0022146510383501.

6. Leah Campbell, "How 'Mommy Juice' Culture Is Normalizing Alcohol Addiction," accessed September 7, 2023, https://www.healthline.com/health-news/the-rise-of-mommy-juice-culture-and-its-impact-on-kids.

7. Trish Elizabeth, "Around the Carousel," unpublished manuscript, 58–59.

8. U.S. Department of Health and Human Services, "National and State Estimates of Children Living with Parents Using Substances, 2015–2019," accessed September 5, 2023, https://aspe.hhs.gov/reports/children-living-parents-using-substances.

9. Rosemary O'Connor. *A Sober Mom's Guide to Recovery* (Minnesota: Hazelden Press, 2015): 179.

10. Ibid., 179–80.

11. Anna Lembke, *Dopamine Nation: Finding Balance in an Age of Indulgence* (New York: Dutton, 2021), quote from back cover.

12. Ibid., 47–57.

13. *The Social Dilemma,* directed by Jeff Orlowski (Argent Pictures and Exposure Labs, 2020), 1:23:45, https://www.netflix.com/title/81254224.

14. Y. S. Lee, D. H. Han, S. M. Kim, and P. F. Renshaw, "Substance Abuse Precedes Internet Addiction," *Addictive Behaviors* 38 no. 4 (April 2013):2022–2025. https://doi:10.1016/j.addbeh.2012.12.024.

15. *The Social Dilemma*, 1:05:39.

16. Lembke, *Dopamine Nation*, 191.

17. *The Social Dilemma*, 55:17.

18. Ibid., 55:45.

19. Social Work Today, "Researchers Find Link Between Excessive Screen Time and Suicide Risk," accessed September 12, 2023, https://www.socialworktoday.com/news/dn_121317.shtml.

20. S. C. Curtin and M. F. Garnett, "Suicide and Homicide Death Rates Among Youth and Young Adults Aged 10-24: United States, 2001-2021," Center for Disease Control and Prevention, *National Center for Health Statistics (NCHS) Data Brief* 471 (June 2023):1–8.

21. J. M. Twenge, T. E. Joiner, M. L. Rogers, and G. N. Martin, "Increases in Depressive Symptoms, Suicide-Related Outcomes, and Suicide Rates Among U.S. Adolescents After 2010 and Links to Increased New Media Screen Time," *Clinical Psychological Science* 6, no. 1 (2018): 3–17, https://doi.org/10.1177/2167702617723376.

22. Surgeon General, "Social Media and Youth Mental Health," the U.S. Surgeon General's Advisory 2023, accessed September 14, 2023, https://www.hhs.gov/surgeongeneral/priorities/youth-mental-health/social-media/index.html.

23. *The Social Dilemma*, 51:17.

24. Ibid., 1:20:20.

25. Surgeon General, "Social Media and Youth Mental Health."

26. American Psychological Association, "Health Advisory on Social Media Use in Adolescence," accessed September 14, 2023, https://www.apa.org/topics/social-media-internet/health-advisory-adolescent-social-media-use.

27. Ibid.

Chapter 10: Recovery Pride

1. Bud Mikhitarian, *Many Faces, One Voice: Secrets from The Anonymous People* (Las Vegas: Central Recovery Press, 2015), 225.

2. Merriam-Webster.com, "Shame," accessed September 19, 2023, https://www.merriam-webster.com/dictionary/shame.

3. Brené Brown, *Daring Greatly: How the Courage to Be Vulnerable Transforms the Way We Live, Love, Parent and Lead* (New York: Gotham Books, 2012), 58.

4. Anna Lembke, *Dopamine Nation: Finding Balance in an Age of Indulgence* (New York: Dutton, 2021), 207.

5. E. Bilevicius, A. Single, L. A. Bristow, M. Foot, M. Ellery, M. T. Keough, and E. A. Johnson, "Shame Mediates the Relationship Between Depression and Addictive Behaviors," *Addictive Behaviors* 82(2018):94–100, https://doi.org/10.1016/j.addbeh.2018.02.023.

6. Cindy House, *Mother Noise* (New York: Marysue Rucci Books/Scribner, 2022), 48.

7. Brené Brown, *Daring Greatly*, 75.

8. Ibid., 79.

9. Anna Lembke, *Dopamine Nation: Finding Balance in an Age of Indulgence* (New York: Dutton, 2021), 216–224.

10. Alcoholics Anonymous, *Alcoholics Anonymous* (New York: Alcoholics Anonymous World Services, Inc. 2001), 562.

11. Bud Mikhitarian, *Many Faces, One Voice*, 109.

12. Josie Feliz, "Survey: Ten Percent of American Adults Report Being in Recovery from Substance Abuse or Addiction," accessed September 25, 2023, https://drugfree.org/newsroom/news-item/survey-ten-percent-of-american-adults-report-being-in-recovery-from-substance-abuse-or-addiction/.

13. Bud Mikhitarian, *Many Faces, One Voice*, 102.

14. Ibid., 103.
15. Ibid., 213.
16. Jason Roop, "Addiction and Leadership: How Authentic and Transformative Leaders are Emerging from the Adversity of Substance Use Disorder," *Journal of Addiction Therapy and Research* 6 (2022):10–23.
17. Ibid.
18. Ernest Kurtz and Katherine Ketcham, *The Spirituality of Imperfection*, 111.
19. Ibid.
20. Ibid., 138.
21. Ibid., 19.
22. Ibid., 112.
23. Substance Abuse and Mental Health Services Administration, "National Recovery Month 2023," accessed September 24, 2023, https://www.samhsa.gov/recovery-month.
24. Bud Mikhitarian, *Many Faces, One Voice*, 282.
25. Brené Brown, *Daring Greatly*, 74–75.
26. Ibid., 80–82.
27. Kristen Neff, "Self-Compassion," accessed September 25, 2023, https://self-compassion.org/the-three-elements-of-self-compassion-2/.
28. Chris Germer, "About," accessed September 25, 2023, https://chrisgermer.com/about/.
29. Sarah Allen Benton, *Understanding the High-Functioning Alcoholic: Breaking the Cycle and Finding Hope* (Lanham, MD: Rowman & Littlefield Publishers, 2009), 162.

Bibliography

Alcoholics Anonymous World Services, Inc. *Daily Reflections.* New York: Simon & Schuster, 1990.

American Psychological Association. "Health Advisory on Social Media Use in Adolescence." Accessed September 14, 2023. https://www.apa.org/topics/social-media-internet/health-advisory-adolescent-social-media-use.

American Psychological Association. "Stress in the Time of COVID-19." *Stress in America,* May 2020, Vol. 1. https://www.apa.org/news/press/releases/stress/2020/report.

American Society for Reproductive Medicine. "Waiting to Have a Baby? Don't Wait Too Long." Accessed July 26, 2023. https://www.reproductivefacts.org/news-and-publications/fact-sheets-and-infographics.

Bartle-Haring, S., N. Slesnick, and A. Murnan. "Benefits to Children Who Participate in Family Therapy with Their Substance-Using Mother." *Journal of Marital and Family Therapy 44*, no. 4 (2018): 671–86. https://doi:10.1111/jmft.12280.

Baumrind, D. "Current Patterns of Parental Authority." *Developmental Psychology* 4, no. 1 (1971): 1–103. https://doi: 10.1037/h0030372.

Baumrind, D. "The Influence of Parenting Style on Adolescent Competence and Substance Abuse." *Journal on Early Adolescence* No. 11 (1991): 56–95. https://doi:10.1177/0272431691111004.

Beattie, Melody. *Codependent No More.* Center City, MN: Hazelden Press, 1992.

Benson, Herbert and Eileen M. Stuart. *The Wellness Book: The Comprehensive Guide to Maintaining and Treating Stress-Related Illness.* New York: A Fireside Book, 1992.

Benton, Sarah Allen. *Understanding the High-Functioning Alcoholic: Breaking the Cycle and Finding Hope.* Lanham, MD: Rowman & Littlefield Publishers, 2009.

Bilevicius, E., A. Single, L. A. Bristow, M. Foot, M. Ellery, M. T. Keough, and E. A. Johnson. "Shame Mediates the Relationship Between Depression and Addictive Behaviors." *Addictive Behaviors* 82 (2018):94–100. https://doi.org/10.1016/j.addbeh.2018.02.023.

Brené Brown, *Daring Greatly: How the Courage to Be Vulnerable Transforms the Way We Live, Love, Parent and Lead.* New York: Gotham Books, 2012.

Brownell, Rachel. *Mommy Doesn't Drink Here Anymore.* San Francisco, CA: Conari Press, 2009.

Campbell, Leah. "How 'Mommy Juice' Culture Is Normalizing Alcohol Addiction." Accessed September 7, 2023. https://www.healthline.com/health-news/the-rise-of-mommy-juice-culture-and-its-impact-on-kids.

Center for Disease Control and Prevention. "Depression During and After Pregnancy." Accessed August 24, 2023. https://www.cdc.gov/reproductivehealth/features/maternal-depression/.

Center for Disease Control and Prevention. "End of Federal COVID-19 Public Health Emergency (PHE) Declaration." Updated May 5, 2023. https://www.cdc.gov/coronavirus/2019-ncov/your-health/end-of-phe.html.

Clark, Diana. *Family Healing Strategies* workbook. Self-Published, 2008.

Cleveland Clinic. "Substance Use Disorder (SUD)." Accessed August 1, 2023. https://my.clevelandclinic.org/health/diseases/16652-drug-addiction-substance-use-disorder-sud.

Cohen, L. S., L. L. Altshuler, B. L. Harlow et al. "Relapse of Major Depression During Pregnancy in Women Who Maintain or Discontinue Antidepressant Treatment." *Journal of the American Medical Association* 295, no. 5 (2006):499–507. https://doi:10.1001/jama.295.5.499.

Cohut, Maria. *Medical News Today.* Accessed September 5, 2023. https://www.medicalnewstoday.com/articles/what-are-the-health-benefits-of-friendship#Connection-matters,-but-its-not-about-numbers.

Columbia University Department of Psychiatry. "How Sleep Deprivation Impacts Mental Health." Updated March 16, 2022. https://www.columbiapsychiatry.org/news/how-sleep-deprivation-affects-your-mental-health.

Connecticut Community for Addiction Recovery. *Recovery Coach Academy* curriculum, 2015.

Cross, R. and K. Dillon. "The Hidden Toll of Microstress." *Harvard Business Review,* February 7, 2023. https://hbr.org/2023/02/the-hidden-toll-of-microstress.

Csikszentmihalyi, Mihaly. *Flow: The Psychology of Optimal Experience.* New York: Harper-Perennial, 1991.

Cucinotta, D. and M. Vanelli. "WHO Declares COVID-19 a Pandemic." *Acta Biomedica* 91, no. 1 (March 19, 2020):157–60. https://doi: 10.23750/abm .v91i1.9397.

Curtin, S. C. and M. F. Garnett. "Suicide and Homicide Death Rates Among Youth and Young Adults Aged 10–24: United States, 2001–2021." *National Center for Health Statistics (NCHS) Data Brief* 471 (June 2023):1–8.

Czeisler, M. É. et al. "Mental health, Substance Use, and Suicidal Ideation During the COVID-19 Pandemic—United States, June 24–30, 2020." *Morbidity and Mortality Weekly Report* 69 (2020):1049–1057. http://dx.https://doi .org/10.15585/mmwr.mm6932a1external icon.

Dayton, Tian. *Emotional Sobriety: From Relationship Trauma to Resilience and Balance*. Florida: Health Communication, Inc., 2007.

Deak, J. D. and E. C. Johnson. "Genetics of Substance Use Disorders: A Review." *Psychological Medicine* 51, no. 13 (October 2021):2189–2200. https:// doi: 10.1017/S0033291721000969.

Divine, A., C. Blanchard, C. Benoit, D. S. Downs, and R. E. Rhodes. "The Influence of Sleep and Movement on Mental Health and Life Satisfaction during the Transition to Parenthood." *Sleep Health* 8, no. 5 (2022): 475–83. https:// doi.org/10.1016/j.sleh.2022.06.013.

Doss, B. D. et al. "The Effect of the Transition to Parenthood on Relationship Quality: An Eight-Year Prospective Study." *Journal of Personality and Social Psychology* 96, no. 3 (2009): 601–19.

Elizabeth, Trish. "Around the Carousel." Unpublished manuscript, used with permission.

Ettman, C. K. et al. "Persistent Depressive Symptoms During COVID-19: A National, Population-Representative, Longitudinal Study of U.S. Adults." *The Lancet Regional Health—Americas* 5 (2022). https://doi.org/10.1016/j .lana.2021.10009.

Germer, Chris. "Center for Mindful Self-Compassion." Accessed September 25, 2023. https://chrisgermer.com/about/.

Gibran, Kahlil. *The Prophet*. New York: Random House, 1997.

Gill, Karen. "Maternal Instinct: Does it Really Exist?" Healthline.com. April 23, 2020. https://www.healthline.com/health/parenting/maternal-instinct#is-it -a-myth.

Graham, Jaydee. *The Soul Grind*. Los Angeles: Launch Pad Publishing, 2021.

Grant, B. F. and D. A. Dawson. "Age at Onset of Alcohol Use and Its Association with DSM-IV Alcohol Abuse and Dependence: Results from the National Longitudinal Alcohol Epidemiologic Survey." *Journal of Substance Abuse* 9 (1997):103–10.

Grose, Jessica. *Screaming on the Inside: The Unsustainability of American Motherhood*. New York: Mariner Books, 2022.

Holt-Lunstad, J., T. B. Smith, and J. B. Layton. "Social Relationships and Mortality Risk: A Meta-analytic Review." *PLOS Medicine* 7, no. 7 (2010). https://doi.org/10.1371/journal.pmed.1000316.

Horigian, J. E. et al., "Long-Term Effects of Brief Strategic Family Therapy for Adolescent Substance Users." *Drug and Alcohol Dependence* 140 (2014): e91.

House, Cindy. *Mother Noise*. New York: Marysue Rucci Books/Scribner, 2022.

Jorquez, J. "The Retirement Phase of Heroin Using Careers." *Journal of Drug Issues* 18, no. 3 (1983): 343–65.

Kelly J. F. et al., "Prevalence and Pathways of Recovery from Drug and Alcohol Problems in the United States Population: Implications for Practice, Research, and Policy," *Drug Alcohol Depend* 181, no. Supplement C (2017): 162–69, https://doi.org/10.1016/j.drugalcdep.2017.09.028.

Kessler, R. C., L. Adler, R. Barkley et al. "The Prevalence and Correlates of Adult ADHD in the United States: Results from the National Comorbidity Survey Replication." *American Journal of Psychiatry* 163 (2006):716–23.

Khantzian, Edward J. and Mark Albanese. "The Self-Medication Hypothesis of Substance Use Disorders: A Reconsideration and Recent Application." *Harvard Review of Psychiatry* 4, no. 5 (1997): 231–44.

Khantzian, Edward J. and Mark Albanese. *Understanding Addiction as Self-Medication*. Lanham, MD: Rowman and Littlefield, 2008.

King, Chrissy. "Self-Care Is an Act of Survival." Accessed June 20, 2023. https://www.girlsgonestrong.com/blog/articles/self-care-act-survival/.

Kuppens, S. and E. Ceulemans. "Parenting Styles: A Closer Look at a Well-Known Concept." *Journal of Child and Family Studies* 28, no. 1 (2019): 168–81. https://doi: 10.1007/s10826-018-1242-x.

Kurtz, Ernest and Katherine Ketcham. *The Spirituality of Imperfection: Storytelling and the Search for Meaning*. New York: Bantam Books, 1992.

Lander, L., J. Howsare and M. Byrne. "The Impact of Substance Use Disorders on Families and Children: from Theory to Practice." *Social Work in Public Health* 28, no. 3–4 (2013):194–205. https://doi: 10.1080/19371918.2013.759005.

Leach, L. S., C. Poyser, A. R. Cooklin and R. Giallo, "Prevalence and Course of Anxiety Disorders (and Symptom Levels) in Men Across the Perinatal Period: A Systematic Review." *Journal of Affective Disorders* 190 (Jan 2016): 675–86.

Lebrun-Harris, L. A. et al. "Five-Year Trends in US Children's Health and Well-Being, 2016–2020." *Journal of the American Medical Association Pediatrics* 176, no. 7 (2022). https://doi:10.1001/jamapediatrics.2022.0056.

Lee, Y. S., D. H. Han, S. M. Kim, and P. F. Renshaw. "Substance Abuse Precedes Internet Addiction." *Addictive Behaviors* 38, no. 4 (April 2013):2022–2025. doi: 10.1016/j.addbeh.2012.12.024.

Lembke, Anna. *Dopamine Nation: Finding Balance in an Age of Indulgence*. New York: Dutton, 2021.

Luthar, S. S. and L. Ciciolla, "What it Feels Like to Be a Mother: Variations by Children's Developmental Stages." *Developmental Psychology* 52, no. 1 (January 2016):143–54. https://doi: 10.1037/dev0000062.

Marschall, A. "What Is Bowenian Family Therapy?" Accessed June 20, 2023. https://www.verywellmind.com/bowenian-family-therapy-definition-and-techniques-5214558.

Martínez, N. et al. "Self-Care: A Concept Analysis." *International Journal on Nursing Sciences* 8, no. 4 (2021): 418–25. https://doi: 10.1016/j.ijnss.2021.08.007.

Merriam-Webster Dictionary. Accessed September 23, 2023. https://www.merriam-webster.com/dictionary/.

Meyers, Robert and Brenda Wolfe, *Get Your Loved One Sober: Alternatives to Nagging, Pleading, and Threatening.* Center City, MN: Hazelden Publishing, 2004.

Mikhitarian, Bud. *Many Faces, One Voice: Secrets from The Anonymous People.* Las Vegas: Central Recovery Press, 2015.

Minkin, Rachel and Juliana Menasce Horowitz. *Parenting in America Today: A Survey Report (2023) Pew Research Center.* Accessed August 22, 2023. https://www.pewresearch.org/social-trends/2023/01/24/parenting-in-america-today/.

Morgan, T., N. Uomini, L. Rendell et al. "Experimental Evidence for the Co-Evolution of Hominin Tool-Making Teaching and Language." *Nature Communications* 6, no. 6029 (2015). https://doi.org/10.1038/ncomms7029.

National Institute of Health, National Institute on Drug Abuse. "Common Comorbidities with Substance Use Disorders Research Report, Part 1: The Connection between Substance Use Disorders and Mental Illness." Accessed August 1, 2023. https://nida.nih.gov/publications/research-reports/common-*comorbiditie4.s*-substance-use-disorders/part-1-connection-between-substance-use-disorders-mental-illness.

National Institute of Health, National Institute of Alcohol Abuse and Alcoholism. "Genetics of Alcohol Use Disorder." Accessed May 14, 2023. https://www.niaaa.nih.gov/alcohols-effects-health/alcohol-use-disorder/genetics-alcohol-use-disorder.

National Institute of Health, National Institute on Alcohol Abuse and Alcoholism. "The Link Between Stress and Alcohol." *Alcohol Alert* No. 8 (2012): 3–4.

Neff, Kristen. "Self-Compassion." Accessed September 25, 2023. https://self-compassion.org/the-three-elements-of-self-compassion-2/.

Nichols, M. and R. Schwartz. *Family Therapy: Concepts and Methods.* Boston: Pearson Education Company, 2001.

O'Farrell, T. J., and K. Clements, "Review of Outcome Research on Marital and Family Therapy in Treatment for Alcoholism." *Journal of Marriage and Family Therapy* 38, no. 1 (2012): 122–44. https://doi:10.1111/j.1752-0606.2011.00242,

O'Connor, Rosemary. *A Sober Mom's Guide to Recovery.* Center City, MN: Hazelden Press, 2015.

Orlowski, Jeff. *The Social Dilemma.* Argent Pictures and Exposure Labs, 2020. 1 hr., 34 min. https://www.netflix.com/title/81254224.

Panchal, N. et al. "The Implications of COVID-19 for Mental Health and Substance Use." *Kaiser Family Foundation Issues Brief.* Updated February 10, 2023 and March 20, 2023. https://www.kff.org/coronavirus-covid-19/issue-brief/the-implications-of-covid-19-for-mental-health-and-substance-use/.

Paulson, J. F. and S. D. Bazemore. "Prenatal and Postpartum Depression in Fathers and Its Association with Maternal Depression: A Meta-Analysis." *Journal of the American Medical Association* 303, no. 19 (May 2010):1961–1969. https://doi: 10.1001/jama.2010.605.

Pietrzak, R. H., R. B. Goldstein, S. M. Southwick, and B. F. Grant, "Prevalence and Axis I Comorbidity of Full and Partial Posttraumatic Stress Disorder in the United States: Results from Wave 2 of the National Epidemiologic Survey on Alcohol and Related Condition." *Journal of Anxiety Disorders 25* (2011): 456–65. https://doi:10.1016/j.janxdis.2010.11.010.

Pollard, M. S., J. S. Tucker, and H. D. Green. "Changes in Adult Alcohol Use and Consequences During the COVID-19 Pandemic in the US." *Journal of the American Medical Association Network Open* 3, no. 9 (2020): https://doi:10.1001/jamanetworkopen.2020.22942.

Qu, L. and R. Weston. "Opinions of Parents on the Acquisition of Parenting and Relationship Skills." *Family Matters: Australian Institute of Family Studies* 81 (2009): 55–57.

Roop, Jason. "Addiction and Leadership: How Authentic and Transformative Leaders are Emerging from the Adversity of Substance Use Disorder." *Journal of Addiction Therapy and Research* 6 (2022):10–23.

Rosenström, T. H. and F. A. Torvik. "Social Anxiety Disorder Is a Risk Factor for Alcohol Use Problems in the National Comorbidity Surveys." *Drug and Alcohol Dependence* 1, no. 249 (August 2023). https://doi:10.1016/j.drugalcdep.2023.109945.

Saxbe, D. E., et. al. "Fathers' Decline in Testosterone and Synchrony with Partner Testosterone During Pregnancy Predicts Greater Postpartum Relationship Investment." *Hormones and Behavior* 90 (April 2017) 39–47. doi: 10.1016/j.yhbeh.2016.07.005.

Senior, Jennifer. *All Joy and No Fun: The Paradox of Modern Parenting.* New York: HarperCollins, 2014.

Social Work Today. "Researchers Find Link Between Excessive Screen Time and Suicide Risk." Accessed September 12, 2023. https://www.socialworktoday.com/news/dn_121317.shtml.

Study.com. "Family Systems Types, Benefits and Examples." Accessed July 26, 2023. https://study.com/learn/lesson/family-system-types-examples.html.

Substance Abuse and Mental Health Services Administration. "Age of Substance Use Initiation among Treatment Admissions Aged 18–30." *The TEDs Report July 17, 2014*. https://www.samhsa.gov/data/sites/default/files/WebFiles_TEDS_SR142_AgeatInit_07-10-14/TEDS-SR142-AgeatInit-2014.htm.

Substance Abuse and Mental Health Services Administration. "Behavioral Health Trends in the United States: Results from the 2014 National Survey on Drug Use and Health." Rockville, MD: Center for Behavioral Health Statistics and Quality, Substance Abuse and Mental Health Services Administration, 2015. https://www.samhsa.gov/data/sites/default/files/NSDUH-FRR1-2014/NSDUH-FRR1-2014.pdf.

Substance Abuse and Mental Health Services Administration. "Key Substance Use and Mental Health Indicators in the United States: Results from the 2020 National Survey on Drug Use and Health." Rockville, MD: Center for Behavioral Health Statistics and Quality, Substance Abuse and Mental Health Services Administration, 2021. https://www.samhsa.gov/data/.

Substance Abuse and Mental Health Services Administration. "National Recovery Month 2023." Accessed September 24, 2023. https://www.samhsa.gov/recovery-month.

Substance Abuse and Mental Health Services Administration. "Recovery and Recovery Support." Accessed May 10, 2023. https://www.samhsa.gov/find-help/recovery.

Substance Abuse and Mental Health Services Administration. "Results from the 2013 National Survey on Drug Use and Health: Summary of National Findings." Rockville, MD: Substance Abuse and Mental Health Services Administration: 2014.

Substance Abuse and Mental Health Services Administration. "SAMHSA Announces National Survey on Drug Use and Health (NSDUH) Results Detailing Mental Illness and Substance Use Levels in 2021." Accessed May 15, 2023. https://www.samhsa.gov/newsroom/press-announcements/20230104/samhsa-announces-nsduh-results-detailing-mental-illness-substance-use-levels-2021.

Substance Abuse and Mental Health Services Administration. *Substance Use Disorder Treatment and Family Therapy. Treatment Improvement Protocol (TIP) Series no. 39*. Rockville, MD: Substance Abuse and Mental Health Services Administration, 2020.

Surgeon General. "Social Media and Youth Mental Health. The U.S. Surgeon General's Advisory 2023." Accessed September 14, 2023. https://www.hhs.gov/surgeongeneral/priorities/youth-mental-health/social-media/index.html.

Szymanski, Jeff. *The Perfectionist's Handbook: Take Risks, Invite Criticism, and Make the Most of Your Mistakes*. Hoboken, NJ: Harvard Health Publications, 2011.

Terlizza, E. P. and J. S. Schiller. "Estimates of Mental Health Symptomatology, by Month of Interview: United States, 2019." National Center for Health Statistics, March 2021.

Tolle, Eckhart. *The Power of Now: A Guide to Spiritual Enlightenment.* Novato, CA: New World Library, 1999.

Twenge, J. M., T. E. Joiner, M. L. Rogers, and G. N. Martin. "Increases in Depressive Symptoms, Suicide-Related Outcomes, and Suicide Rates Among U.S. Adolescents After 2010 and Links to Increased New Media Screen Time." *Clinical Psychological Science* 6, no. 1 (2018): 3–17. https://doi.org/10.1177/2167702617723376.

Twenge, J. M., W. K. Campbell, and C. A. Foster. "Parenthood and Marital Satisfaction: A Meta-Analytic Review." *Journal of Marriage and Family* 65, no. 3 (2003): 574–83.

Umberson, D. and J. K. Montez. "Social Relationships and Health: A Flashpoint for Health Policy." *Journal of Health and Social Behavior* 51 Supplement (2010): S54–66. https://doi: 10.1177/0022146510383501.

U.S. Bureau of Labor Statistics. "Women in the Labor Force: A Databook." Accessed July 26, 2023. https://www.bls.gov/cps/cps_over.htm.

U.S. Department of Health and Human Services. "National and State Estimates of Children Living with Parents Using Substances, 2015–2019." Accessed September 5, 2023. https://aspe.hhs.gov/reports/children-living-parents-using-substances.

Valenti, Jessica. *Why Have Kids: A New Mom Explores the Truth About Parenting and Happiness.* New York: New Harvest Houghton Mifflin Harcourt, 2012.

Van der Kolk, Bessel. *The Body Keeps Score: Brain, Mind, and Body in the Healing of Trauma.* New York: Viking, 2014.

Weiss, Roger and Hilary Smith Connery. *Integrated Groups Therapy for Bipolar Disorder and Substance Abuse.* New York: Guilford Press, 2011.

White, W. and E. Kurtz. "The Varieties of Recovery Experience." *International Journal of Self Help and Self Care* 3, no. 1–2 (2006): 21–6.

Wilson, Bill. "Emotional Sobriety." Accessed August 4, 2023. https://barricks.com/AASayings/emotional.html.

Wisner, K. L. et al. "Onset Timing, Thoughts of Self-Harm, and Diagnoses in Postpartum Women with Screen-Positive Depression Findings." *JAMA Psychiatry* 70, no. 5 (May 2013): 490–98. doi: 10.1001/jamapsychiatry.2013.87.

Index

About the Author

Sarah Allen Benton is a licensed professional counselor and advanced alcohol and drug counselor. She is co-owner of Benton Behavioral Health Consulting, specializing in clinical and business support services. Sarah is also co-founder and the chief clinical officer for Waterview Behavioral Health, an intensive outpatient program for mental health in Wallingford, Connecticut. She has held a clinical director and several primary therapist positions, including at McLean Hospital in Belmont, Massachusetts. Sarah is a popular public speaker and teaches continuing education courses internationally for behavioral health professionals on the treatment of substance use disorders and other clinical topics. She has been in recovery from alcohol use disorder since February 2004 and uses her own story to increase awareness and fight the associated stigma. She has been featured in the *New York Times* and appeared on *The Oprah Winfrey Show*, *CBS Early Show*, *The Today Show*, SiriusXM, NPR, and writes a Psychologytoday.com blog called *The High-Functioning Alcoholic*. Sarah has personally and professionally observed the challenges that parents in recovery face and wrote this book to provide a relatable resource. This is her second book on the topic, following the 2009 publication of *Understanding the High-Functioning Alcoholic*. Sarah lives in Killingworth, Connecticut, with her husband and daughter. Sarah's website is www.bentonbhc.com